COMFORT ONE

ANOTHER

Trish Dukes

New Harbor Press
Rapid City, SD

New Harbor Press
1601 Mt Rushmore Rd, Ste 3288
Rapid City, SD 57701
www.newharborpress.com

Ordering Information:
Quantity sales. Special discounts are available on quantity purchases by corporations, associations, and others. For details, contact the "Special Sales Department" at the address above.

Comfort One Another/Dukes —1st ed.

ISBN 978-1-63357-426-7

First edition: 10 9 8 7 6 5 4 3 2 1

To my beloved husband, Billy aka Billdog;

*To my precious sons and the wonderful
daughters they gave me;*

*To my beautiful grandchildren who I adore and
are the crown of my old age;*

*To my cookie sister, my dearest friend, and
brother Butch;*

*To my awesome, loving, generous brothers and
the sweet sisters they gave me who I am so
blessed to share life with;*

To all my dear family and friends; and,

*To all those who need comfort, hope,
encouragement and peace . . .*

This is for you.

Contents

INTRODUCTION

It is with great joy that I share God's Word and my heart with you!

I come to you as a daughter, a sister, a wife, a mother, a grandmother, a friend. But my most important title is a child of the Most High God! Without Him, my story would definitely not be one of hope.

I'll start with an explanation of the cover, because it's the reason for everything that follows.

The Lord led me many years ago to begin a women's Bible study in my home. What followed were many days of seeking His heart on the truths He wanted me to share with my sisters and daughters in the Lord. There were times my inspiration came from my quiet times with the Lord. But there were other times I felt no inspiration and I would fall to my knees asking Him what His girls desperately needed to hear that week. Each time, without fail, He would lay a word on my heart. Sometimes, it would be one Bible verse. Other times, it would be to incorporate my own experiences along with the Word.

One day, I was sitting in my recliner praying over an upcoming Bible study when the Lord gave me a vision. The first picture was of a woman on her back with Satan's foot on her neck. The second picture was of a woman of God reaching out to help her up and take her eyes off the enemy. The third picture was of the two women joining hands and looking to Heaven, to the Savior Who had been there all the time. Those three pictures He placed so clearly in my mind told me this was His call on my life and on the lives of those who belong to Him. And that vision came straight from the Word: "Blessed be the God and Father of our Lord Jesus Christ, the Father of mercies and God of all comfort, Who comforts us in all our tribulation, that we may be able to comfort those who are in any trouble, with the comfort with which we ourselves are comforted by God." (2 Corinthians 1:3–4)

The apostle Paul was telling us that his comfort in suffering came straight from the Lord Jesus, which enabled him to bring comfort to others who were suffering. How desperately we need one another in this life which sometimes brings much sorrow!

When Satan knocks us down with relentless blows and we feel helpless, we need a brother or sister in Christ to come alongside us, take our gaze off the enemy of our soul, give us a hand, and point us again to the One Who saves. The ONLY One Who saves.

As Christ's followers, we must allow the Holy Spirit to comfort us and bring us into all truth, and in turn, pass that comfort and truth along to others. Each day, our Lord Jesus, our Savior and perfect example, spent time alone with the Father, and then went out and spoke truth and hope and comfort to those who would listen. And so we must do.

The pages that follow are a compilation of the studies the Lord has given me over the years. My deepest prayers are this:

If you do not know Him as Savior, you will run into His loving arms.

If you belong to Him, you will fall more in love with Him each day.

That my words and my stories will bring hope and comfort to all who read. And point you to the Cross!

May He alone be glorified!

1 – HOW TO BUILD A "POWER" HOUSE

1 Corinthians 3:9–11—You are God's building. According to the grace of God which was given to me, as a wise master builder I have laid the foundation and another builds on it. But let each one take heed how he builds on it. For no other foundation can anyone lay than that which is laid, which is Jesus Christ.

I was sixteen years old when I first felt the urging of the Holy Spirit on my heart. Our church was having a revival and the pastor had given an altar call. No doubt I had heard many altar calls before, being a pastor's daughter, but this time was different. This time, my heart was pounding and tears were falling. I KNEW that Jesus was calling me to serve Him. And to walk to that altar and respond. And I did.

I remember kneeling there praying, repenting, and telling Jesus I wanted to serve Him. And a pastor came by and prayed for me. I didn't realize it that day because of my youth, but in later years, I learned the simple, but profound, truth: that Jesus MUST be our foundation. And from the day we give our life and heart to Him, we are building on that foundation in one way or another.

As we know, the strength of any house is in its foundation, and the stability of that house is totally dependent on its foundation. When we are saved, we become the temple of God (1

Corinthians 3:16–17), and Jesus, as our foundation, is where our strength comes from.

The Bible uses another word for foundation and that is *cornerstone*. It is defined as a stone uniting walls, the chief foundation on which something is built, something that is essential and indispensable. In ancient times, the cornerstone was the first stone set in a masonry foundation. It was the strongest, the largest, the most expensive, and the most important stone because it bound the walls together. The strength of the entire building was dependent upon this first stone and it had to be perfectly level, because every other stone that was laid would conform to the shape of the cornerstone. Do you see the beautiful, perfect correlation here to our precious Lord Jesus, the perfect cornerstone? Glory to God for painting such an easy picture for us to take hold of!

In Psalm 118:22, Matthew 21:42, and 1 Peter 2:6, Jesus was actually referred to as the elect, precious, chief cornerstone which the builders rejected. The builders were the church leaders of Jesus' day, and by rejecting Him, they destroyed their "spiritual house" by destroying the only true spiritual foundation.

Jesus spoke of this in Matthew 7:24–27 when He told the Parable of the Wise and Foolish Builders. He said that whoever hears His words and obeys them is like a wise man who built his house on the rock (Jesus). When the rain, winds, and floods came and beat on that house, his house did not fall because it was founded on the rock. But whoever hears His words and fails to obey them is like a foolish man who built his house on the sand (anything or anyone but Jesus). When the rains, winds, and floods came and beat on that house, his house fell, and its fall was great. Jesus made it clear that we all will face attacks, trials, and adversities in life, but with Him as our foundation, we can and will endure every storm!

Jesus wants to be our foundation! The strongest, the sweetest, the best! Salvation is not the end; it's the beginning of our spiritual journey! So where do we go from there? We build from our foundation with a house plan. And that is the Bible!

Psalm 119 is a wonderful chapter on the importance of knowing God's Word and keeping His commandments. The cry of our heart should be verses 33–35. "Teach me, O Lord, the way of Your statutes, and I shall keep it to the end . . . Make me walk in the path of Your commandments, for I delight in it." And verse 11, "Thy Word I have hid in my heart that I might not sin against Thee." And verse 105, "Your Word is a lamp unto my feet and a light unto my path." His Word will guide our steps and show us the path we are to walk on. Hebrews 4:12 tells us that the Word of God is living and powerful and sharper than a two-edged sword. And 1 Peter 2:2 says that we are to desire the pure milk of the Word, that we may grow thereby.

As we seek our Lord by reading the Word in an effort to know Him and His heart and His plans for us, He reveals them to us "through His Spirit. For the Spirit searches all things, yes, the deep things of God." (1 Corinthians 2:10) So in building terms, we could call the Holy Spirit the lead contractor in building our power house!

We then build our "spiritual house" daily by the choices we make. As the Holy Spirit brings us into all truth, we choose to either obey His voice or to disobey. 1 Peter 2:4–5 says that "Coming to Him as a living stone, rejected indeed by men, but chosen by God and precious, you also (us), as living stones, are being built up into a spiritual house, a holy priesthood, to offer up spiritual sacrifices acceptable to God through Jesus Christ."

When we choose to place stones of obedience, forgiveness, mercy, patience, self-sacrifice, joy, kindness, hope, peace, righteousness, purity, and holiness, we are building upon the foundation that was laid with the precious blood of our Savior, a house that is so pleasing to our Father, and as that perfect cornerstone that Jesus is, we are being conformed to His image! Praise His Name!

So, all that's left is the mortar that will bind our house together. Clearly, LOVE is the mortar that binds. Colossians 3:4 actually says that love is the bond of perfection. The word *love* appears 314 times in the King James Version of the Bible. There is no bond greater than love. Jesus Himself told us this when asked what the greatest commandment was. And in 1 Corinthians 13, we are told that without love, we are nothing, and that love is the greatest gift we must desire, because God IS love. We can never forget that "God SO LOVED the world that He gave His only Son . . . ." It was all for love the Savior came.

Have you ever seen a brick house where the mortar is cracked and breaking? The bricks fall apart because there is nothing to hold them together. That's us without love. A brick is nothing without mortar, and the Bible says we are nothing without love.

As we build our lives, our spiritual houses, on the foundation that is Jesus and we follow the Holy Spirit's leading, placing those living stones upon that foundation and binding them together with love, we are not only building our spiritual house, but drawing others to Him and helping them build their houses as well. As humanity, we are drawn to those who exhibit peace and joy and hope in the midst of "rains, winds, and floods." Because it is unnatural and impossible to face deep adversity and continue to be strong on our own. It is only through the power of the Holy Spirit that we can face those storms and stand.

Jesus is our strength and our strong foundation.

The Bible is our house plan.

Holy Spirit is our lead contractor.

And love is the mortar that binds: the love He sheds abroad in our heart through the Holy Spirit.

If you haven't made Jesus your foundation, please don't go any further until you do! The Bible is so clear that unless we are born again, we cannot enter the Kingdom of Heaven (John 3:3). And Jesus is the ONLY way to the Father (John 14:6). I KNOW it is true. He is real and loves you so. And so do I.

And, if He is your Savior, but that mortar is beginning to crack, go back to your foundation. Go to Him right now and ask Him to forgive you and restore the love, the mortar that binds your spiritual house together. I promise you that He will!

Now you are ready to go forward and hold fast and keep building on your foundation! Our precious Savior!

2 – PRAYER

Luke 11:1-2 "Lord, teach us to pray . . ." So He said to them, "When you pray, say: Our Father in Heaven, hallowed be Your Name. Your kingdom come, Your will be done . . . ."

What is *prayer* but communication with our God? Did you know that it's a word that pertains only to Him, a word that in the original Hebrew meant "to judge oneself"? What does that mean? I think it means that when we pray, when we commune with Him, in the presence of the one, true Holy God, we cannot pretend. In His Presence, we can only see ourselves as He sees us!

If you look at the Lord's Prayer, it consists of praise, petition, and repentance. It's the perfect guide to how we should pray, and we know that because the Lord Jesus Himself was the Teacher.

As a little girl, our family always had nightly prayer altars. We all knelt by the couch and took turns praying, ending with the Lord's Prayer together. In my young mind, I thought prayer was only to tell Jesus that I loved Him, and then to ask Him for something. When I grew up and realized my need for a Savior, He taught me that my relationship with Him is BUILT on my communication with Him, one of which is prayer. He commanded us in 1 Thessalonians 5:17 to "pray without ceasing." For me, that means praying when I wake up, before I even open my eyes; setting aside a special time to pray before starting my day; praying throughout the day; and, praying until I fall asleep each night.

Before we proceed, let's look at what the Word tells us are hindrances to our prayers.

The first one is unforgiveness and is found in Mark 11:24–26. We are told that we MUST forgive others if we are to be forgiven. It's not always easy, but we can choose to forgive, even as Jesus has forgiven us.

Another hindrance to prayer is sin and disobedience. Psalm 66:18 says, "If I had cherished sin in my heart, the Lord would not have listened." I'll be very transparent here and say something that's difficult, but must be said. I see people on social media commenting that they will be praying for the need of a friend. And, sadly, I know some of these people are not saved. The Bible is clear that we will know who belongs to Jesus by the fruit of their life. God's Word makes it clear that He does not hear the prayers of the unsaved, unless it is a prayer of repentance. (Job 9:31, Proverbs 1:26–29, Proverbs 28:9, John 9:31, 1 Peter 3:12)

Unbelief is also a hindrance, as spoken of in Matthew 21:22. We are told in all things we ask in prayer, we must believe in order to receive.

So, before we pray about anything, let's examine our hearts and be sure there is no unforgiveness, sin, or unbelief that rules us. And if there is, let's repent FIRST!

And, as we pray for ourselves, we are also instructed to pray for others. Are we willing to be prayer warriors for Jesus? A Christian soldier as the old song says? When someone is hurting, are we afraid to go to them and pray with them? We are commanded to confess our sins to each other and to pray for each other so we may be healed in James 5:16, followed by a promise that the prayer of a righteous person is powerful and effective.

Over thirty years ago, I remember hearing the Holy Spirit tell me to go and pray for a friend who was terminally ill with cancer. Even though I was saved, I was young in the Lord and in my walk with Him. I was terrified! And, along with that command, there came a physical weight on my chest. It was so heavy it was almost unbearable. But with all that, I still hesitated. I told the Lord for two days that I just didn't think I could do it.

Finally, the weight was just too much. I drove up to my friend's house almost in a trance of fear. The Lord had asked something of me that was impossible. Or so I thought. I knocked on the door and my friend's mom answered. I took my friend a gift, a picture of Jesus that was mine; He was standing at a gate covered with beautiful roses. I remember telling her that it had brought me peace and I wanted her to have it. We visited for a while, and finally, I asked her if I could pray with her. She said I could, and so I did. As I was leaving, her mom followed me to the door and down the steps. As I turned around, she fell into my arms weeping. Here's what she said to me: "Thank you so much for coming! We have been so discouraged and needed a word of hope. Thank you for bringing that to us today." Wow. There she was, waiting for someone to bring comfort and hope. And to think I almost didn't go because I was worried about *myself*.

The Lord taught me a valuable lesson that day: When He gives us a command, we MUST obey. 1 John says that if we love Him, we keep His commandments. My error was in thinking I had to go in my own power. I didn't know at the time what the Word says: that we do not have to plan ahead of time what we say, but we must submit to Holy Spirit and let Him lead us. And that's what happened when I submitted myself to Him that day.

During that time, I was fortunate to be in a Bible study with an older woman of God, along with two friends who were my age. Her name was Joan Simmons, and she taught us so much about being a godly woman. She was so gentle, so kind, so understanding, so willing to help when we were in a crisis in life. She taught us never to say, "I will pray for you," but instead, "Let's pray right now." We never met for a Bible study that we did not call on the name of the Lord for a very long, long time! As our spiritual mentor, she truly taught us to pray.

I will get off course for just a moment and share a funny, but telling story about my friend, Ms. Simmons. We went to the same church and always ended each service with prayer at the altar. On one particular evening, we were all at the altar praying. Ms. Simmons was praying for someone when her half-slip suddenly fell down around her ankles! I would have died in embarrassment, but not Ms. Simmons. She was close to the front pew, so she just kicked it under the pew and kept praying! Isn't that awesome? Her life wasn't about her, it was about Jesus and others, so it was just not a big deal. We all laughed about it afterward, thinking about her great humility and sense of humor. As I write this, she is with her Beloved Savior, reaping her most beautiful reward.

A few years later, I was at another friend's house at a Bible study. This friend had lost her son in a tragic accident only months before. As the study was coming to a close and prayer requests mentioned, the young man's grandmother (who was also in attendance) began to weep. She shared that she had not been able to move past the sorrow and despair of losing her grandson. The lady sitting next to her patted her arm and said she would be praying for her. But the Holy Spirit said to me in very clear words, "Pray for her NOW." This time, I hesitated only a few seconds before asking her, "Can we pray for you now?" Her reply, "Please do!" We surrounded that precious grandmother, laid hands on her, and prayed for the peace of Almighty God to come upon her. We prayed for the peace that passes all understanding to be hers right then, in Jesus' powerful Name. When the prayer was done, she smiled through her tears, hugged me, and said she already felt better!

So, why do we hesitate when the Holy Spirit speaks? Because the more we obey Him, and obey Him speedily, the easier it becomes! Today, thirty years later, I stand ready, actually looking for others to pray for in their times of need because I KNOW the power of prayer. My favorite Old Testament verse is this (2

Chronicles 16:9) and I quote it each time I pray for someone: "The eyes of the Lord look to and fro across the whole earth to show Himself strong on behalf of those whose heart is loyal to Him." Don't you love that? What a promise!

One day, a friend knocked at my door. She was devastated because she had just received a report that her daughter possibly had cancer. We sat down together and talked and then held hands to pray. As we prayed, I heard the sound of wind and a felt a presence with us. The sound was so loud, I thought someone had come into the room, but I did not open my eyes. When we finished praying and opened our eyes, there was no one else there. I knew the Lord wanted us to know how close He was to us as we were seeking Him! Her daughter's report came back and was negative for cancer. Praise be to His great Name! And from that encounter with my friend, the Holy Spirit directed me to go through the Bible and list page after page of God's promises for we who believe. I still have that list and I will share it with you, too, so that you can remember and hold fast to these promises!

So when we pray, let's repent, let's praise, let's petition, let's believe, and let's give thanks to our wonderful Savior Who stands ready to hear and to answer us, His children.

GOD'S PROMISES

Philippians 4:6–7—Be anxious for nothing, but in everything by prayer and supplication, with thanksgiving, let your requests be made known to God. And the peace of God, which surpasses all understanding, will guard your heart and your mind in Christ Jesus.

Psalm 103:1–5—Bless the Lord, O my soul; and all that is within me, bless His holy Name. Bless the Lord, O my soul, and forget not all His benefits: Who forgives all your iniquities, Who heals all your diseases, Who redeems your life from destruction, Who crowns you with loving-kindness and tender mercies, Who satisfies your mouth with good things, So that your youth is renewed like the eagles.

Isaiah 54:17—No weapon formed against you shall prosper and every tongue which rises against you in judgment, you shall condemn.

Isaiah 26:3—You will keep him in perfect peace whose mind is stayed on You, because he trusts in You. Trust in the Lord forever, for in Yah, the Lord *is* everlasting strength.

Psalm 107:20—He sent his Word and healed them.

Isaiah 30:19—He will be very gracious to you at the sound of your cry; when He hears it, He will answer you.

2 Chronicles 16:9—For the eyes of the Lord run to and fro throughout the whole earth, to show Himself strong on behalf of those whose heart is loyal to Him.

1 John 5:14—Now this is the confidence that we have in Him, that if we ask anything according to His will, He hears us. And if we know that He hears us, whatever we ask, we know that we have the petitions that we have asked of Him.

Hebrews 6:18—It is impossible for God to lie.

Romans 3:4—Let God be true but every man be a liar.

Hebrews 4:16—Let us therefore, come boldly to the throne of grace, that we may obtain mercy and find grace to help in time of need.

Psalm 120:1—In my distress, I cried to the Lord and He heard me.

Jeremiah 29:11—For I know the thoughts I think toward you, says the Lord, thoughts of peace and not of evil, to give you a future and a hope.

Psalm 138:8—The Lord will perfect that which concerns me.

Psalm 41:1–3—Blessed is he who considers the poor; the Lord will deliver Him in time of trouble. The Lord will preserve him and keep him alive, and he will be blessed on the earth . . . The Lord will strengthen him on his bed of illness; You will sustain him on his sickbed.

Deuteronomy 30:20—Love the Lord your God . . . obey His voice . . . cling to Him, for He is your life and the length of your days.

Psalm 20:6—Now I know that the Lord saves His anointed; He will answer him from His holy heaven with the saving strength of His right hand.

Psalm 91:4—Because he set his love upon Me; therefore, I will deliver him.

2 Samuel 21—The Lord was my support. He delivered me because He delighted in me.

John 16:23—Whatever you ask the Lord in My Name, He will give you.

John 16:33—In the world you will have tribulation; but be of good cheer, I have overcome the world.

Proverbs 18:21—Death and life are in the power of the tongue and those who love it will eat its fruit.

Proverbs 17:22—A merry heart does good, like medicine.

Isaiah 50:2—Is my Hand shortened at all that it cannot redeem? Or have I no power to deliver?

1 Thessalonians 5:16–18—Rejoice always, praying without ceasing, in everything giving thanks, for this is the will of God in Christ Jesus for you.

Ezra 8:22 and 31—The Hand of our God is upon all those FOR GOOD who seek Him. And the Hand of our God was upon us and He delivered us.

Proverbs 30:5—Every word of God is pure; He is a shield to those who put their trust in Him.

1 John 4:18—There is no fear in love, but perfect love casts out all fear. But he who fears has not been made perfect in love. We love Him because He first loved us.

Revelation 12:11—They overcame by the blood of the Lamb and the word of their testimony.

Ephesians 1:17–19—That the God of our Lord Jesus Christ . . . may give to you the spirit of wisdom and revelation in the knowledge of Him, the eyes of your understanding being enlightened, that you may KNOW the hope of His calling . . . And the exceeding greatness of His power toward us who believe . . . ."

Isaiah 53:4–5—Surely He has borne our griefs and carried our sorrows . . . But he was wounded for our transgressions, He was bruised for our iniquities, the chastisement for our peace was upon Him, and by His stripes we are healed.

Proverbs 3:1–4—Do not forget My law, But let your heart keep my commands, for length of days and long life and peace they will add to you.

Matthew 8:1–17—Speak a word, and my servant will be healed . . . As you have believed, so let it be done for you . . . with a word, He healed all who were sick.

1 Peter 2:24—Who Himself bore our sins in His own body on the tree, that we, having died to sins, might live for righteousness—by whose stripes you were healed.

Isaiah 49:15–16—Can a woman forget her nursing child, and not have compassion on the son of her womb? Surely they may forget, Yet I will not forget you. See, I have inscribed you on the palms of My Hands.

2 Corinthians 10:3–6—For though we walk in the flesh, we do not war according to the flesh. For the weapons of our warfare are not carnal but mighty in God for pulling down strongholds, casting down arguments and every high thing that exalts itself against the knowledge of God, bringing every thought into captivity to the obedience of Christ, and being ready to punish all disobedience when your obedience is fulfilled.

Psalm 34—I will bless the Lord at all times; His praise shall continually be in my mouth . . . Oh magnify the Lord with me, and let us exalt His Name together. I sought the Lord and He heard me, and delivered me from all my fears. They looked to Him and were radiant . . . The angel of the Lord encamps all around those who fear Him, and delivers them . . . Many are the afflictions of the righteous, But the Lord delivers him out of them all.

Psalm 46:1–2—God is our refuge and strength, a very present help in trouble. Therefore we will not fear.

Mark 11:22–24—So Jesus answered and said to them, "Have faith in God." For assuredly I say to you, whoever says to this mountain, "Be removed and be cast into the sea," and does not doubt in his heart, but believes that those things he says will be done, he will have whatever he says. Therefore I say to you, whatever things you ask when you pray, believe that you receive them, and you will have them.

Psalm 91—He who dwells in the secret place of the Most High shall abide under the shadow of the Almighty. I will say of the Lord, "He is my refuge and my fortress; My God, in Him will I trust." Surely He shall deliver you from the snare of the fowler and from the perilous pestilence. He shall cover you with His feathers, and under His wings you shall take refuge. His truth shall be your shield and buckler. You shall not be afraid of the terror by night, nor of the arrow that flies by day, nor of the pestilence that walks in darkness, nor of the destruction that lays waste at noonday. A thousand may fall at your side and ten thousand at your right hand; but it shall not come near you. Only with your eyes you shall look and see the reward of the wicked. Because you have made the Lord, who is my refuge, even the Most High, your dwelling place, no evil shall befall you, nor shall any plague come near your dwelling. For He shall give His angels charge over you, to keep you in all your ways. In their hands they shall bear you up lest you dash your foot against a stone . . . Because he has set his love upon Me, therefore, I will deliver him. I will set him on high, because he has known My Name. He shall call upon Me, and I will answer him; I will be with him in trouble; I will deliver him and honor him. With long life I will satisfy him, and show him My Salvation.

3 – FORGIVENESS

Matthew 6:14–15—"For if you forgive other people when they sin against you, your heavenly Father will also forgive you. But if you do not forgive others their sins, your Father will not forgive your sins."

Whether we have been saved a day or a decade, offering someone the gift of forgiveness is sometimes a difficult struggle, especially if we have embraced it for a long time. So how do we walk in love and forgiveness and not offense?

First of all, what exactly does it mean to *forgive*? It is defined as the act of granting a pardon, cancelling a debt, ceasing to feel resentment against, releasing or redeeming.

In Jesus' words in the parable in Matthew 18:21–35, He explains the importance of forgiveness perfectly. It begins when Peter asks the Master how many times he must forgive someone who wrongs him. He asks Jesus, "Seven times?" And He replies, "Not seven times, but seventy times seven." To illustrate why, Jesus tells a parable about an unforgiving servant. The servant owes the king $2,250,000,000 (in today's dollar) and when the servant is unable to pay, the king orders he and his family imprisoned. When the man begs the king to forgive the debt, the king shows mercy and forgives it all *because he realizes it is a debt greater than he will ever be able to pay.* But that same servant goes to another man who only owes him $2,000 and demands his money. When he is unable to pay the debt, he has him thrown in prison. The king finds out and has the servant brought before him and throws him in prison until the debt is paid.

The verses referenced above tell us something that should stop us in our tracks: Jesus says the way the king treated the unforgiving servant is how our Heavenly Father will treat us if we don't forgive.

This is the way God sees it: He sent His precious, beloved Son to die for us and forgave us so much—it was a debt that we could not pay. Holding onto offenses from others is simply not acceptable to the Father after He has forgiven us so much more than we will ever have to forgive others.

When we refuse to forgive someone, when we hold onto a wrong someone has done to us, it is described in the Word in Hebrews 12:15 as "a root of bitterness that defiles." *Root* is defined as the essential, main, primary organ of a plant that anchors it to the ground, so we know that a root is very strong. *Bitterness* is defined as disagreeable, sour, and hostile. So a root of bitterness in us would be when our primary attitude has become one of negativity, agitation, irritation.

I was in the greenhouse business for ten years, and was so blessed to see one spiritual truth after the other played out before me in the growing of plants.

There was a large shrub sitting outside the greenhouse door that had a weed in it. I walked by that plant every day and every day said I needed to stop and pull that weed. But I was so busy with all my other tasks I continued to pass it by. One day I realized the weed had gotten huge, so I finally stopped to pull it out and was amazed that it wouldn't budge! I had to take the plant out of the pot and get a knife and cut part of the dirt and root system out to get the root of that weed! I was able to save the plant but it had to undergo surgery! It seems that weeds grow faster than anything else.

This is an exact picture of what unforgiveness does to us. First, it's small. But if it's not dealt with quickly, it grows fast and takes over. This is why Jesus said in Ephesians 4:26, "Don't let the sun go down on your wrath." Because He knows that unforgiveness leads to anger and to bitterness and will not stop growing until it is removed; it will eventually consume! Unforgiveness is poison!

There was a lady that used to come into my greenhouse all the time. She had suffered what she perceived as a wrong decision at the hands of a judge and actually had a wooden plaque made and affixed to the back of her car that outlined the wrong. It always made me sad to know that this wrong had so overtaken her that she had become obsessed by it. She was defined by this wrong and not able to release it. She probably went to her grave thinking about it every moment and never asking forgiveness or being forgiven. I hope I'm wrong.

Sometimes, our unforgiveness is as visible as that poor lady's was. But, other times, we can hide it from others for a time, like the mums I grew one fall.

They were slowly growing and blooms were emerging. But, one day as I was watering them, I noticed a dark spot underneath the outside leaves. As I pushed back the greenery and the blooms, I saw that the undergrowth was black! I began to check them all and saw that every single one was affected! The mums clearly had a disease that was about to kill them from the roots up. I was horrified because the mums represented my fall income. I treated them with a fungicide to no avail. Then, I decided to call on that dear mentor friend referenced in a previous chapter, Ms. Simmons, to come and pray over my mums! So, us four Bible Study girls stood in that mum patch and agreed with her prayers as she called on the name of Jesus to please heal and save my mum crop! And guess what? He did!

It is the same with us: When we allow the sin of unforgiveness to grow, it will eventually take over and destroy. Just like my mums were destined to do until the power of the Savior's Name entered the scene! Praise His Holy, Powerful Name!

Paul told us in Hebrews 12:1–2,

"Let us lay aside every weight, and the sin which so easily *ensnares* us, and let us run with endurance the race that is set before us, looking unto Jesus, the author and finisher of our faith, who for the joy that was set before Him endured the cross, despising the shame, and has sat down at the right hand of the throne of God."

A *snare* is simply a trap. And God told us not to be ignorant of Satan's devices in 2 Corinthians 2:11.

Satan always has and always will try to trap us who belong to Jesus with offense and unforgiveness because he knows how deadly it is in our lives. We are to run the race, keep our eyes on the prize which is Jesus, not look to the right or to the left, but look unto Him. This is the Word. What that means is this: If someone offends us, we quickly say, "I forgive you," and keep running that race. But what do most of us do? We stop, gasp, and say, "OMG, did you hear what she just said to me?" And we tell it and retell it and retell it and it gets bigger every time, and the more we tell it, the more stirred up we get! In the plant comparison, this is *fertilizing a weed*! I wish I could tell you I read about these types of responses in a book! But, unfortunately, by the time you get my age, there are few situations you have not walked. I suppose this is why our Great God said for older women to teach younger women their wisdom!

I was tested in this very area recently when something I said to a friend caused a reaction from her that blindsided me. She didn't like my response to her comment and lashed out in anger at me. I was shocked that she would be so rude and hurtful. Then I was angry. How dare she attack me verbally like that? I was so angry I was moved to tears, and then decided to tell someone what she had done. But guess what? The Holy Spirit stopped me. Could I choose to forgive instead of maligning her to someone else? I sure didn't want to; I wanted to tell someone what she had said. But if I listened to the Holy Spirit and followed the example set forth by my Savior, I must forgive. And I did. I chose to never tell anyone what she had said to me, and moved on.

Corinthians 13 says that true love suffers long, is not easily offended; that we *cannot* keep a record of wrongs. When we accept Jesus as our Savior, we must begin a life of forgiveness. Galatians 2:20 says, "It is no longer I who live, but Christ who lives in me . . ." so we are to let His love take over, daily let self die and love and react to others like He would.

One day, I was praying and Jesus gave me a beautiful picture of how to easily forgive. He asked me to close my eyes and imagine walking through this life all alone; facing every situation of offense and hurt alone and trying to forgive. Then, He asked me to imagine facing all those same situations, but this time He was actually holding my hand and walking with me through all those things. And, when someone offended me, I would turn to Him and say, "Lord, did You see what she just said to me?" And He would say with a sad smile on His Sweet Face, "I saw, and I know what it's like to be hurt and rejected. But I want you to let it go and forgive, because vengeance is for Me and My Father. Let's just walk in love and joy on this journey TOGETHER!"

This is exactly what His desire is for each one of us: to take our hurts, our wounds DIRECTLY TO HIM. Because no matter what we take to Him, He knows what to do with it. We just have to give it to Him. *He so desires us to* COMMUNICATE WITH HIM! TALK TO HIM IN THE MORNING, AT NOON, AT NIGHT, ALL DAY. AND THEN BE SILENT AND LISTEN TO HIM SPEAK TO YOU, BECAUSE WHEN YOUR BFF IS JESUS, YOU CANNOT, CANNOT HOLD ONTO UNFORGIVENESS!

Jesus Himself showed us what forgiveness looked like when He went to the Cross. Some of His last recorded words were, "Father, forgive them, because they don't realize what they are doing." (Luke 23:24)

This type of forgiveness is unimaginable to us! But it shows us that we MUST FORGIVE EVEN WHEN OUR OFFENDER DOES NOT ASK FOR FORGIVENESS because this is what Jesus did!

Unforgiveness is like a ball and chain that has US bound; not the one who wronged us. When we release an offense, when we forgive, we are free! Forgiving others is for us! The Word says in John 8:36, "He who the Son sets free is free indeed." Thank You, Jesus!

If there is any unforgiveness in your heart, let it go right now. Give it all to Jesus. Let Him make you free. Father, give us a heart like Jesus!

4 – TAKE UP YOUR CROSS

Luke 9:23–24—"If anyone would come after Me, he must deny himself and take up his cross DAILY and follow Me. For whoever wants to save his life will lose it, but whoever loses his life for Me will save it."

At first glance, this doesn't sound like an appealing offer, does it? Deny ourselves? To the contrary, most of us (if we are honest) spend our lives pampering ourselves, don't we?

Most of us love getting our pedicures, manicures, massages, stopping by for that special coffee, binge-watching our favorite shows, staying on Facebook and Instagram, and, my personal favorite, shopping! And, most recently, I've added another favorite and that is baking cookies! I love baking and decorating cookies, especially with my sister! So fun! Yes, we do love those things and would argue that they are good and most definitely have their place in our lives.

The question is this: are we self-focused or are we Jesus-focused?

In these verses from Luke 9, Jesus was talking to his twelve disciples, and had just told them He was about to suffer many things, be killed, and raised the third day. He followed that by telling them what He would require of them and ALL who would choose to follow Him in the future. He was talking about US.

And He was actually using His words to tell them what method of death He was about to suffer. It must never be lost on us that death on a cross was the most shameful, torturous death one could die in Jesus' day. Our precious Savior was destined to die on a cross. And Jesus told us why in John 3:16: "For God so loved the world that He gave His only begotten Son, that whosoever believes in Him, will not perish but have everlasting life." Jesus could have laid down His life in many ways, but the Father *chose* the Cross. And Jesus was willing to do whatever was required to bring us to the Father.

So what does it mean to us today, to *take up our cross*? It's so important that we know the answer and that we choose to obey that command.

First, the Cross of Christ represented His **purpose**. The Cross was the reason He came. He said that He came to seek and to save the lost by His death and resurrection (John 3:17). So *taking up our cross* means fulfilling OUR purpose, the reason WE are on this earth, and that is for a personal relationship and fellowship with Him as our Savior, and then to go and love and make disciples of all men. (Matthew 28:19–20)

We begin the process of fulfilling our purpose when we respond to Him as He knocks at the door of our heart through His Holy Spirit. When we accept Christ as our Savior and choose to walk with Him on the road of righteousness, we must be willing to lay down our right to ourselves. It is a process, for certain, but it is a process that is required.

And Jesus told us in Revelation 3:15–16 that we must be *all in* with Him. Being lukewarm is not acceptable. We must be hot or cold.

Does it surprise you that He actually said it's BETTER to be hot or cold than to be lukewarm?

This came home to me when I was in a backslidden state when I was in my late twenties. As previously mentioned, I had walked an aisle in church when I was sixteen, repented for my sins, and asked Jesus to save me. But, over the years, my love for Him had grown cold and I was again walking in sin. On that particular day, I was at work and heard someone take God's Name in vain. I opened my mouth to ask them to please not do that. Here's what I heard in my mind before I could speak: "Don't defend Me if you are not going to serve Me."

Wow. I had been admonished by the voice of the Holy Spirit. I was so ashamed and I closed my mouth and said nothing.

I later came back to the Lord, and only then understood what had happened that day.

You see, if I had publicly defended the Lord, it would have seemed that I was serving Him. But, clearly, by the life I was living, I was not. And that would only have hurt His Name. In Matthew 15:8, we are told that there are those who honor Him with their lips, but their hearts are far from Him. I am so sorry today that I wasted years that I could have been serving Him! And I am so grateful that His sweet and tender mercies are new every morning!

Secondly, the Cross of Christ represented **death**. He died, that we might live. He died to make a way for us to be forgiven. He died because of His love for us. In John 15:12, He said, "There is no greater love than to lay down one's life for his friends." His earthly life and death were spent walking out obedience to His Father's perfect will. And that is what He requires of us.

We must seek Him, listen to His voice through the Word and prayer, and obey.

Dying to self can be summed up in the words that our Lord Jesus spoke in the Garden of Gethsemane before He went to the Cross: "Not My will, but Yours be done." (Luke 22:42)

Before I came back to the Lord, I was definitely self-focused. I'm ashamed to say that I'd spend up to an hour each night trying on clothes for work the next day. I was so intent on looking my best that I made that my priority each evening. I'd finally settle on the best combination of pieces and lay them out for the next morning. Instead of just being concerned about looking nice, I was clearly obsessed with it.

I was in my early thirties when I stopped and listened to the voice of the Holy Spirit say this: "Choose this day who you will serve." I had been going back and forth by that time, as the saying goes, with one foot in the world and one foot in the church. I remember being afraid, knowing the Lord was telling me it was time to make a decision and not look back. Praise His Holy Name, that day I told Him I was ready, and responded simply with these words: "Lord, please forgive me! I choose *You!*"

From that day to this, I have not looked back. I have fallen down on this road of righteousness many times, to be sure. But I made a decision that day that I will keep my heart and mind focused on Him, daily seeking Him early, and will stay on this path with Him until I breathe my last breath.

Through all the sorrows and sadness that life has brought, that life brings to us all, I cry out to my Jesus, my Savior, my Beloved. Sometimes, I tell Him I don't understand why I or my loved ones are suffering. Sometimes, I ask Him for answers. Sometimes, I get those answers and other times I do not. That is when I tell Him this: "Lord, I do not understand, but I DO trust You." And whatever life brings, I've chosen to fall on the rock which is Jesus, and cling tightly to His Hand.

My choice to put Jesus first resulted in a change in that clothing-obsessed ritual, too. Over time, I found myself just making sure my clothes were washed and at least ready to fluff up the next morning in the dryer before I got ready! You see, my priorities had changed. I still wanted to look my best, but I grew to understand that inner beauty was what mattered most to my Savior: that a gentle and quiet spirit in love with Him was His perfect will (1 Peter 3:4).

So, lastly, as you see, the Cross of Christ represented **life!** Resurrection life! He was raised from the dead that third day and now sits at the right hand of the Father! And He's always making intercession for us! And resurrection life is what awaits *us* on

That Day He takes us to our Heavenly home! Hallelujah! Glory to our Savior's most precious Name!

I've found that the joy of dying to self and living for Jesus is unmatched by any earthly pleasure! The peace and the hope and the very real love He offers is everything to me. His love is the sweetest love you will ever know. He is so worthy of our all. There is no other place I choose to be than *all in* with my Savior!

If you are reading this and have not taken up your cross, I pray that today will be the day you CHOOSE to lay down your right to yourself, and walk in the joy of following Him all the days of your life!

5 – OVERCOMING STRONGHOLDS

2 Corinthians 10:3–5—For though we walk in the flesh, we do not war according to the flesh. For the weapons of our warfare are not carnal, but mighty in God for pulling down strongholds, casting down arguments and every high thing that exalts itself against the knowledge of God, bringing every thought into captivity to the obedience of Christ.

Is there anything in your life that seems to have a "strong hold" on you? Anything that seems to control you?

Before I knew this verse, I was not only susceptible to strongholds, I had allowed strongholds to develop in my life. It's so easy for it to happen, but very difficult to break it. That's why it's so important to understand what it is, how it happens, how to break it, and how to keep it from taking hold again.

Let's start by defining *stronghold*. The dictionary defines a *stronghold* as a well-defended, deeply entrenched, fortified city. In spiritual terms, a *stronghold* is anything or anyone that has taken control or is attempting to take control over us with the result being addiction or obsession. Satan is behind every spiritual stronghold. Examples are alcoholism, gambling, pornography, some relationships, and mindsets (unforgiveness). Strongholds can be so invasive that we become defined by those things.

So, how does a stronghold get established? The Great Deceiver Satan looks for the area or areas in our life where our "armor of God" is not covered—where we are weak and needy. That is usually the place where he begins to tempt and deceive us. There are then three steps in the enemy's establishment of a stronghold in our life.

1. He speaks—we listen. Satan's ploys begin by attacking us through our thoughts. The truth is this: IN ORDER FOR US TO RECOGNIZE THE VOICE OF THE ENEMY, WE MUST KNOW GOD'S WORD, WHICH ENABLES US TO KNOW THE TRUTH AND CAST DOWN LIES. Satan's objective is to twist the Truth of God and make us believe lies. Remember that the Lord will never speak anything to us that does not line up with His Word, so if the voice in our mind contradicts God's Word, then we must know it is the voice of Satan. When he speaks through our thoughts, we must CHOOSE to cast down those thoughts with the Name of Jesus. EVERY STRONGHOLD IS BASED ON A LIE THAT SATAN SPEAKS AND WE BELIEVE. HE IS A LIAR AND THE FATHER OF ALL LIES AND THE TRUTH IS NOT IN HIM! However, if we hold onto those thoughts and listen, step 2 will ultimately follow.

2. We receive and believe what he says. As we continue to focus on and believe the enemy's voice, that voice grows stronger and his words begin to take root in our heart. If we do not take authority over that thought, step 3 WILL happen.

3. We act on what we've heard and believed. This is where the stronghold begins. The more we act on what began as a thought that we failed to take authority over, the more it grows and becomes established and the harder it is to break. Strongholds have the power to control us.

The danger of strongholds is the result. Every addiction, every affair, every suicide, every murder, every obsession began as a thought. IT'S IMPORTANT TO KNOW THE SECRET OF HOW THE ENEMY OF OUR SOUL WORKS SO THAT WE CAN KNOW THE SECRET OF OVERCOMING HIM; the Bible tells us not to be ignorant of Satan's devices. (2 Corinthians 2:11)

So, now to the most important question: How do we break a stronghold once it has been established?

The first step is to have a change of heart and want to let it go. OUR LOVE FOR JESUS MUST BE GREATER THAN OUR LOVE FOR THAT STRONGHOLD. The Lord God created us for fellowship with Him and made a vacuum inside of us that only He could fill and satisfy. Some people spend their entire lives searching for something or someone to fill the emptiness in their souls when only Jesus can fill that place with His Presence and His Peace. Strongholds of any kind infringe on our relationship with Jesus, because we begin to put that addiction/obsession/mindset ahead of Him. It's important to remember, though, that there is no stronghold that can't be broken by the power of His Word IF WE WILL STAND ON HIS WORD AND LET HIM DELIVER US! We have been instructed that we are to fight against Satan's lies with the sword of the Spirit which is the Word of God!

The second step is to pray or get someone we trust to pray with us, to acknowledge our stronghold as SIN and repent, and to cast it down in Jesus' Name. If the stronghold involves a person, we must pray for that person. As we pray, He gives us the strength to release it to Him. We then receive His sweet mercy and forgiveness!

The third step is to lay that stronghold, that person/addiction/mindset at the foot of the Cross. There are times we simply cannot make wrong feelings disappear, but what we can do is give those feelings to Jesus because He knows what to do with them. When Satan tries to bring that stronghold back, we must remind him that the stronghold has been broken and turned over to Jesus and WE WILL NEVER LET IT GET PAST A THOUGHT AGAIN. We have chosen to "take every thought captive to the obedience of Christ" and to trust in the power of God that is unfailing!

And, finally, how do we keep from being susceptible to strongholds again?

"Seek ye first the Kingdom of God and every other need will be supplied" (Matthew 6:33). Give Jesus FIRST PLACE IN YOUR HEART AND EVERY PART OF YOUR HEART, SOUL, MIND, AND STRENGTH (fall in love with Him!). KNOW WHO YOU ARE IN HIM. ONCE WE ARE SAVED AND HAVE ACCEPTED JESUS AS OUR SAVIOR, WE ARE DAUGHTERS/SONS OF THE MOST HIGH GOD AND WE NEED TO ACT LIKE IT! Luke 11:24–26 is the story of a man delivered from an unclean spirit, whose house (heart) was then swept clean (empty). Because his house (heart) was empty and not filled with the Holy Spirit, he was still susceptible to the enemy, who then came back with seven other spirits more wicked than himself, and they entered and dwelled there; and, the last state of that man was worse than the first. WE WILL BE CONTROLLED BY SATAN OR BY JESUS, BUT WE MAKE THE CHOICE!

We need to put on the armor of God every day by beginning our day (firstfruits of your time) in prayer and in the Word. BECAUSE I BELONG TO HIM, I WILL DAILY SEEK HIS FACE.

Now that I know who I am and He is my first love, there is no part of me that is weak, needy, or susceptible to the enemy. When the enemy tries to tempt me, I am not enticed because I am whole and filled with His Spirit. There is no empty place within me.

Now, I can roll every need over to His shoulders and choose to walk in joy (1 Thessalonians 5:16–18) and choose to focus on good things. I can meditate on God's Word and His Promises to us which are unending! Paul said in Philippians 4:8, "Fix your thoughts on what is true and good and right. Think about things that are pure and lovely, and dwell on the fine, good things in others. Think about all you can praise God for and be glad about it."

Do I sound like an expert in this area? Maybe it's because I've walked through this more than once.

The first time involved caring for someone that was not God's choice for me. I had allowed myself to fall in love when I KNEW it was wrong. I was smitten and consumed with love for this person. When I finally repented and realized I must walk away, I felt helpless. I remember telling the Lord that I was willing to walk away, but simply could not stop loving him. So vividly, the Lord impressed upon me that I was to give HIM the love I felt for this person, because He knew what to do with it. I got on my knees, I held my hands out to Him, and I said, "Lord, I give YOU this love that I never should have allowed. Please take it from me. I will not take it back." There were many times those feelings tried to surface again, but each time I said, "No. I gave those to Jesus." And that is how I overcame.

Another time, my stronghold involved finances. Or, should I say, the lack of finances. We were self-employed and our business was suffering badly. We had borrowed until there was no more borrowing. I was absolutely clueless as I began to listen to a voice in my head that the situation was hopeless. I pondered every possible answer and found none. So, when the voice began to say that the only answer was for me to die and my family to get life insurance, I actually listened. I went so far with it that I despaired of life and actually asked the Lord to take me on to Heaven so the mental and emotional torment would end. And, the worst of all? I kept these thoughts to myself. That made the enemy quite happy, I'm sure.

One night I was watching Christian programming when the speaker began to talk about 2 Corinthians 10:3–5. As I listened to that verse, the reality of what had happened to me hit me hard. I realized for the first time that I had been listening to the voice of Satan! I had allowed him to lie to me, telling me that my finances were hopeless, without remedy. I was so shamed that I wept for almost an hour, repenting for my sin. I thanked the Lord for bringing me to the revelation truth of these verses, and I began to pray instead and BELIEVE for an answer to my financial issues. And, the Lord DID bring financial deliverance once I cast down the lies in His Name.

As you've read these words, have you become aware of something that has a stronghold on you? My dear friend, I pray in Jesus' most powerful Name that you will CHOOSE deliverance!

The only stronghold I will allow in my life now is the "strong hold" my Savior has on my heart! I've given Him my heart and my life, and I read His Word and know His Word, and cast down lies as soon as I hear one in my head! No more allowing the enemy to get past step one! I now hold tightly to the Hand of my Savior and I will NEVER let go. He is my life! And, do you know what I've found? The things of this world no longer appeal to me because the peace, the comfort, the joy, the hope I've found in Him is everything I could ever want or need!

The Lord's desire over us is not to be weighted down with worldly problems and situations, but to be free and whole and walking in joy. May you be FREE from all strongholds, may you KNOW Him deeply, and as you experience the Power of His Love, may His Perfect Will be accomplished in your life!

6 – JESUS IS OUR SAVIOR, BUT IS HE OUR LORD?

Luke 6:46—Why do you call me Lord, Lord, but not do what I say?

The title of this chapter might sound like a strange question to you. I know it did to me when I first heard it. My thought was that He is my Savior, so, of course, He is my Lord! But, after further pondering and praying, I knew it was a question that truly needed to be asked. So, let's start by defining a few key words.

Savior is defined as one that saves from danger or destruction. That means Jesus is the ultimate Savior, the perfect Savior. He said He came not to condemn the world, but to save the world (John 3:17). He came to seek and to save the lost (Luke 19:10).

Let's ask ourselves: Is Jesus my Savior? What does that mean? Let's talk about the process of Jesus becoming my Savior.

1. Through the Holy Spirit, I realize that I am a sinner and that only Jesus can save me. (John 6:44)
2. I repent of my sins and ask Jesus to forgive me and make me His own. (1 John 1:9)
3. I am now a new person, made clean by His precious blood! (2 Corinthians 5:17)

So, I now begin my journey on the road of righteousness!

The verse 1 Corinthians 6:19 is now true for us: "We are bought with a price; we are not our own." What was that price? It was the precious, innocent blood of Jesus. "For God SO LOVED the world that He gave His only begotten Son, that whosoever believes in Him will not perish, but have everlasting life!" (John 3:16) Praise His Holy Name!

So, now let's explore the meaning of the word *lord*. It's defined as one having power, control, or authority over others. It is used 346 times in the Bible. That tells us it's pretty important!

There is another biblical word that means the same. It is *master*. I love this word when applied to our Savior and I often praise Him with that word: "You are my Master, my Savior, my King!"

Jesus is our Lord? Is He? LET'S EXAMINE OURSELVES.

Is Jesus truly Lord of our heart? Our heart is where we LOVE; DO WE LOVE HIM ABOVE ALL ELSE? If we do, what would that look like? We would have a loving heart and love others as ourselves, a joyful heart, a thankful heart, a forgiving heart, because if Jesus has control, power, and authority over my heart, I will love and forgive as He does. I read a commentary once that said forgiveness is hard for us because there is something inside of us that wants justice for those who have wronged us, even as we desire mercy for ourselves. How true this is.

Over our time? Do we sit and watch TV for hours? Do we read the Bible to our children and teach them about Him as He commanded in Deuteronomy 11:19? Back in the day, before television and computers, people sat around the supper table and had meals as a family. My Daddy said most of the spiritual lessons he learned came from sitting around the dinner table with his family. By our actions, we teach our children this is the way Christians live. God help us!

Over our money? Do we ask Him before we spend anything or do we complain we have no money after we are careless? Example: If we waste only $0.60 day, 5 days a week, that is $156/year. If we spend $5 a day foolishly, 5 days a week, that is $1,300/year. That's enough to buy groceries for a family for two months. We complain to the Father about our money and we ask Him why He is not blessing our finances. It's because we have not made Him Lord of our finances! If He was, we would not spend foolishly and then blame it on Him. What are His commands regarding money?

1. That every good and perfect gift is from above, and that certainly includes money (James 1:17)
2. That we are to tithe (Malachi 3:10
3. That we are to pay our taxes (Romans 13:7)
4. That we are to help the poor (Proverbs 21:13)

If we fail to do any of those, He is not Lord of our finances and our finances will always be in chaos. The Lord spoke to me directly about my finances once when I was praying, with these words, "I will not bless you contrary to my Word." What does that mean? It means if I am breaking His laws regarding money, His blessing is not upon my money and they will always be a mess until I bring my finances under His Lordship.

Over our possessions? Do we hold tightly to our stuff or would we give it away at His command? Do we treat our possessions, our home, our cars, our clothes, etc., as if they are ours or as if they are His to be used for His glory? Is our stuff more important to us than people? My sister-in-law gave away her wedding ring at the behest of the Holy Spirit. Could we do that? My son, Brandon, shared a message about giving once: He said if your fist is tightly closed, you're not able to receive or give away. But if that hand is open, you're ready and able to do both!

Over our body? Our body is the temple of the living God if we are saved (1 Corinthians 6:19). What would it look like if He truly had power, control, and authority over our bodies? Would we exercise? Would we eat anything we want? Do we intake things we know are going to damage our bodies? Jesus said, if we want to be His disciples, we must *deny ourselves*, take up our cross *daily*, and follow Him (Luke 9:23). Let's ask ourselves: Do we ever deny ourselves anything? Or, does our life consist of overeating and doing what we want when we want?

Over our speech? Do we say anything that pops in our head about others? If Jesus truly was Lord of our speech, if He had power, control, and authority over our speech, would we say the things we do? Did you know there is a word used sixteen times in the Bible called *revile*? Ever heard of that word? I remember reading it and wondering exactly what it meant, especially after I saw that God takes it so seriously that He says we are not to keep company with revilers (1 Corinthians 5:11)! It means to attack someone verbally, to insult, to berate, to condemn. Our precious Jesus was reviled on the Cross. The Bible says we will one day account for every idle word we speak (1 John 4:17). I don't know about you, but that's a scary thought for me! One of my dear sisters-in-law is one who will not say a bad word about anyone, no matter what. I once was trying to tell her something negative about a relative and she refused to make any comment on the situation whatsoever! It was a short conversation! But it taught me a valuable lesson on reviling.

Over our mind? Do we allow the enemy to put bad thoughts in our mind and discourage us and bring us down? Do we focus on bad situations? Or, do we let Jesus be Lord over our minds and focus on Him above all else? Are we letting Him transform our mind as He said He must do so that we love what He loves and hate what He hates (Romans 12:2)? Are we reading the Word daily so that we even know what His heart and mind are? Jesus said that man does not live by bread alone, but by EVERY WORD that proceeds from His mouth (Matthew 4:4). Does that not mean that we are to KNOW what He has spoken to us?

Our words say yes, Jesus is Lord of my heart, my time, my finances, my possessions, my speech, my mind, but our actions sometimes say He is not. I am convinced that we will never live in victory in any of these areas until we allow Him to be Lord over every area. God set in motion a concept He calls *sowing and reaping*. He says it is such a powerful concept that He will not be mocked regarding this (Galatians 6:7). So, that means if we sow foolishness in our finances, we cannot reap financial blessing. That, if we sow nothing in time and teaching our children about Jesus, we are not going to reap Godly children.

The purpose of this self-examination is not to beat ourselves up. People don't get saved and get perfect. *Sanctification* is a process where God brings about holiness and change in our lives conforming us, transforming us, over time to the image of Jesus. I am most definitely still a work in progress!

My pastor son, Brian, tells a story of a man who invites Jesus to come live in his house in a beautiful room prepared for Him. Satan comes knocking at the man's door, comes in and beats him up, and leaves, and the man asks Jesus why He didn't help him. Jesus tells him that he has only made Him Lord of a room, not Lord of the house. When Satan comes knocking the second time, Jesus answers the door and Satan says that he must have the wrong house because, now, the man has made Jesus Lord of his whole house. This is what happens when we don't allow Jesus to be Lord of all: we try to fight Satan alone in those areas and we just cannot and will not win.

So, am I saying that we must monitor every facet of our life, and heap on more rules and regulations? No! To the contrary! The beauty of relinquishing control and letting Jesus be Lord over every area of our life is this: We only *submit to His authority, listen to His voice* when His Holy Spirit speaks to our heart, and we simply *obey*. We just LET HIM BE LORD.

I try to never start my day without my quiet time of prayer, praise, reading the Bible, and telling my Jesus these words: "I am Yours; use me for Your Glory today!" Because I am something special? No! It's because the only sweet and lasting peace I have ever found is in submitting to the Lordship of the One Who loves me more than anyone else; to the One Who created me, Who died for me, and Who ever lives sitting at the right hand of the Father, praying for me and for us all! (Romans 8:34)

We must remember that His way is the best way for us; that His decisions are always the wisest and will result in blessing. Once we choose to submit to His power and control and authority, all we have to do is listen and obey. That is freedom! If you've not already, I pray you will make the choice to let Him be Lord of All today!

7 – AT HIS FEET

John 8:2–6—Now early in the morning He came again into the temple, and all the people came to Him; and He sat down and taught them. Then the scribes and Pharisees brought to Him a woman caught in adultery. And when they had set her in the midst, they said to Him, "Teacher, this woman was caught in adultery, in the very act. Now Moses, in the law, commanded us that such should be stoned. But what do You say?" This they said, testing Him, that they might have something of which to accuse Him.

She was caught in the very act. I can't begin to imagine the shame.

I've envisioned the Temple scene from this story in John 8 many times. And it will surprise you to hear that it's one of my favorite stories in the New Testament. Why? Read on and you'll see.

Here was Jesus teaching in the Temple when the holier than thou, full of pride scribes and Pharisees set this woman at His feet. They clearly wished to kill two birds with one stone as they publicly accused her of an adulterous act. (A pun to be sure.) They wished to trick Jesus and then follow up with stoning her.

I wonder what they thought Jesus would say or do? Had their previous interactions with Him given them a glimpse of His heart of mercy? Did they believe He would be torn between following the Law and letting her go free?

An observation of the scene would no doubt tell us that her head was hung in shame. She was probably terrified that her life was about to end. Fear and shame. A horrible combination.

I'm sure she had heard of Jesus and wondered what his verdict of her would be. If He was indeed the Savior, would he not be compelled to follow the Law of Moses?

Ah, but there was no way she could have known that she was being judged by the One Who alone makes all things new. The One Who said that He came not to judge but to save! (John 12:47)

And so, instead of replying to their questions of her fate, the Giver of Life simply stooped down and wrote with His finger on the ground. (We can only surmise what He wrote. Many have suggested it could have been their sins?) Then, He said: "Let he who is without sin cast the first stone." One by one they walked away, from the oldest to the youngest. It's not to be missed that their conscience convicted them. Not the Holy Spirit. Sadly, their rejection of Jesus had quenched His work in their lives. (Mark 2:28–30)

As she stood there trembling, little did she know she'd been thrown at the feet of the only One who could save her life. Both physically and spiritually. Just as we are safe in His arms, she was safe at His feet. In His presence. No one could have touched her without His permission. And I just love that.

Can you relate? Have you ever sinned and it became public knowledge? It's one thing to sin secretly and feel shame. But, when everyone knows, it could become almost unbearable.

Shame can take us many places. It can take us into despair. It can take us into deep depression. It can take us into isolation. It can take us into many kinds of addiction. But there is a wonderful place shame can take us and that is to the Cross.

Here's the precious part of this story. The Savior would go on to die for our sin AND our shame. The shame imposed upon

Him as He was stripped and spat upon and His beard plucked? Unimaginable, horrific shame and pain. Breaks me down when I even think of it. But He chose obedience to the Father over His own will.

So, how did this story end? Jesus looked at her and asked where her accusers were. And she told him there were none. And here's the best, the very best, part of the story: "Neither do I accuse you. Go and sin no more."

Wow! She was forgiven of a crime that, according to the Law of Moses, required the penalty of being stoned to death. How could it be?

Jesus was bringing about a new covenant. He was teaching them that all had sinned and come short of God's glory. And that, if we would accept Him as Savior and confess our sins, He would be faithful and would forgive our sins and make us clean. (1 John 1:9) She was pronounced clean and forgiven by Jesus when the scribes and Pharisees had pronounced her dirty and guilty.

And, don't miss this: The shame that the scribes and Pharisees were imposing upon her was turned around and applied to THEM! It was shame that made them walk away!

I'm convinced Jesus saw her heart. And that she was not only ashamed but repentant. And that was enough.

Is there a past sin in your life that still brings you shame? Does Satan bring it to your mind often to torment you? I've most certainly been there. But, once again, there's the promise of our Savior to us: "If any man be in Christ, he is a new creature. Old things have passed away. Behold all things have become new." (2 Corinthians 5:17) All things new.

Do you see now why I love this story? Because I see such mercy, such grace, such love, and such forgiveness extended to this sinful woman instead of the letter of the Law. I see proud, boastful pretenders confounded by the perfect wisdom of Jesus. And, I see the power of what His love can do which I happen to know personally.

That old Trish girl? Did you know her at fifteen? At twenty? At twenty-five? At thirty? Well, she's gone. She was made new! And, even though she's a far cry from perfect, she is definitely a new and different person, praise God! She belongs to the One Who showed mercy to the woman in this story. And to her.

Only the power of almighty God through the blood of Jesus and the wooing of the Holy Spirit can transform a lost, broken, shameful, sad being into a saved, whole, joyful child of the King! Believe it. I'm living proof!

And, until we take our last breath, or until He comes to take us home, may we remain at His feet where His love and mercy always reside!

8 – FAITH LIKE ABRAHAM

Romans 4:20–24—He did not waver through unbelief regarding the promise of God, but was strengthened in his faith and gave glory to God, being fully persuaded that God had power to do what He had promised. This is why "it was credited to him as righteousness." The words "it was credited to him" were written not for him alone, but also for us . . . who believe in Him Who raised Jesus our Lord from the dead.

We first read of a man named Abram in Genesis 11, as the generations of men are listed. But, over in the next chapter, we read that God spoke to him to leave his country and journey to another land. God made a covenant promise to him that He would bless him and multiply his family greatly if he would obey.

I'm sure Abram had many questions, beginning with how his family could be multiplied when his wife, Sarai, was old and barren. But he didn't ask anything of the Lord. The Scriptures do not record Abram questioning the Lord at all. He simply took his own and departed as God had commanded. That is called FAITH.

Faith is defined as complete trust or confidence in someone or something, a firm belief in something for which there is no proof. The Bible defines *faith* like this, from Hebrews 11:1: "Now faith is confidence in what we hope for and assurance about what we do not see." Clearly, Abram had faith in the One Who had spoken to him!

And, here in Romans 4, Paul is encouraging US to be strong like Abram, whose name God later changed to *Abraham*. God had given him promises, but everything he actually looked upon and saw went against those promises ever being fulfilled. Paul is reminding us that Abraham could have doubted God's promises, but instead "he did not waver through unbelief."

So, how can we have faith like Abraham?

The first thing Abraham did was believe. He believed God when He gave him a promise.

The second thing Abraham did was obey. He took his belongings and began his journey.

The third thing Abraham did was give God glory. And, as he gave glory to God, he grew strong in his faith. So beautiful! We believe. We obey. We praise!

In order to be strong in our faith like Abraham, it takes choices. It takes action! We must choose to stand on what we know, not on what we see. Just because we are saved, we are not automatically going to grow strong in our faith.

Our daily prayers should be straight from the Word, straight from the Promise Maker/the Promise Keeper: "Thank You for loving me, for dying on the Cross for me; thank You for promises to never leave me or forsake me; thank You for walking with me when I pass through the fires of life; thank You that I can do all things and endure all things through Christ Who is my strength; and, thank You for Your mercies that never come to an end, that are new every morning!"

Now, that's a faith-growing prayer!

As I was studying Abraham's faith, the Lord actually gave me an illustration, a picture to go with this! Here's what I saw:

Two girls were in the ocean. The first one can't enjoy being in the ocean because of the waves. Her eyes are always on the waves, and she lives in dread of the next one, knowing it's coming. And, it's true: She barely gets up from one before the other one comes and knocks her down. Her life is a perpetual state of being knocked down. And her focus is to just keep from drowning, to just keep her head above water. She can't help save anyone else who might be drowning, because it's all she can do to save herself.

But then there's the girl who put on a life preserver. She's in that same ocean. She's splashing and laughing and enjoying herself. She knows the waves are coming, but decides not to focus on them because even though they may knock her down, they can't drown her because she's got on her life preserver. So, she decides to just have fun and enjoy the ocean. And she's able to help someone else who might be drowning because she's protected.

Obviously, life is that ocean. And, what about the girls and the life preserver?

The first girl represents two possibilities. Maybe she is an unbeliever who has yet to come to Christ for salvation. Or, maybe she's a believer, but a babe in Christ who has yet to overcome fear and is weak in the faith. She has yet to take hold of complete faith and trust in her Savior and is still walking most days in fear.

The second girl is the one who is saved and whose primary focus and first love is Jesus. She reads the Word and knows the Word and is, thereby, enabled to daily stand on God's promises with a thankful heart. She knows life is full of hard times, but embraces her Savior and His great and mighty love for her, knowing He will "work all things together for her good."

But, the life preserver is not just our salvation. Remember, there are those Christians who are weak in the faith and there are those who are strong in the faith. Paul talks about those who are babes in Christ, immature Christians. He never says they are not saved. He says their choices have kept them from maturing in Christ (1 Corinthians 3:1–3).

That life preserver is that choice we talked about earlier. The second girl "put on" that life preserver. She "put on" her faith, her confidence, that's been built because of the relationship she's chosen to build with her Savior. The result is her sure confidence in Christ alone and that the waters will not overtake or overcome. Isaiah 43:2–3 tells us, "When you go through deep waters, I will be with you. When you go through rivers of difficulty, you will not drown . . . For I am the Lord your God, your Savior."

Faith in Him does not say He will never allow us to suffer.

Faith in Him says He will always be with us, that we will never walk alone. Because it is in the fires that we are refined, that we are made to hold fast to Him, that we become more like Him.

Back to those girls in that ocean. I've been both of them over the years. I've lived in almost constant fear of what a day can bring, worrying and fretting over situations out of my control. I've lived getting up early, running and slinging to get ready for my day, swatting the flies of life as they come, and falling out exhausted at the end of the day from the weight of it all. Then, getting up the next morning to do it all again. Madness.

And then I learned about that life preserver. I had a sister in the Lord who told me she got up early every single morning, starting her day with her quiet time with Jesus. It was her special time alone with the Savior in prayer, praise, and the Word. I observed her gentle and quiet spirit and realized that it was a by-product of her faith. And I not only wanted that, I needed that! I was desperate for that!

Now, I start my day with Jesus. I make a full pot of coffee and sit down with my Bible and read and talk to my Savior. I tell Him all my heartaches, all my wounds, I ask Him to heal my heart when it's broken, I ask Him to help me forgive those who wrong me, I pray for my family and friends, for my husband and my children and my grandchildren, I praise His Holy Name. I talk to Him like a friend. Like a dearest, closest friend. Because He is. And then, I end with this: "Lord, use me for Your glory today."

Jesus wants us to enjoy life. He said, "Come unto Me, all you who are heavy laden, and I will give you rest" (Matthew 11:28).

That precious concentration camp survivor, Corrie ten Boom, said it this way:

If you look at the world, you'll be distressed.
If you look within, you'll be depressed.
But if you look at Christ, you'll be at rest.

At rest. Walking in faith. Embracing the Savior and His promises. We have this choice to make:

We can live in a perpetual state of trying to keep our head above water, allowing fear to be our primary emotion.

Or, we, like Abraham, can put on our life preserver and believe, obey, give God the glory, and choose faith and trust in the One Who cannot lie. The One Who will one day come for us and deliver us and take us to our beautiful Heavenly home!

What will you choose today?

9 – IS THE BATTLE REALLY HOPELESS?

2 Kings 6:8–14—Now the king of Syria was making war against Israel; and he consulted with his servants, saying, "My camp will be in such and such a place." And the man of God sent to the king of Israel, saying, "Beware that you do not pass this place, for the Syrians are coming down there." Then the king of Israel sent someone to the place of which the man of God had told him. Thus he warned him, and he was watchful there, not just once or twice. Therefore the heart of the king of Syria was greatly troubled by this thing; and he called his servants and said to them, "Will you not show me which of us is for the king of Israel?" And one of his servants said, "None, my lord, O king; but Elisha, the prophet who is in Israel, tells the king of Israel the words that you speak in your bedroom." So he said, "Go and see where he is, that I may send and get him." And it was told him, saying, "Surely he is in Dothan." Therefore he sent horses and chariots and a great army there, and they came by night and surrounded the city. And when the servant of the man of God arose early and went out, there was an army, surrounding the city with horses and chariots.

Have you ever been in a situation that seemed hopeless? Where there was no possible answer for deliverance other than a miracle? Many times in my life, I've felt this way and, no doubt, you have, too. This is why I love the story found in 2 Kings.

Elisha the prophet had gotten himself in serious trouble with the King of Syria. His prophetic gift had warned the King of Israel of the war plans against him by the King of Syria, prompting him to think there was a traitor in the ranks. So, upon being told that it was not a traitor but a prophet who was confounding his plans, the King of Syria set out to find and destroy Elisha.

Elisha was in a city called Dothan when his servant Gehazi walked outside to see themselves surrounded by the King of Syria's army of soldiers in chariots. They were in a hopeless situation, doomed to death. Or so it seemed.

When Gehazi saw the army, he responded: "Alas, what shall we do?" (*Alas* is a word used to express sorrow, grief, alarm, pending doom, or evil.) Gehazi saw the enemy; he saw hopelessness; he saw death. HE REALIZED THERE WAS NOTHING IN THE PHYSICAL REALM THAT COULD HAPPEN TO SAVE THEM FROM SUCH AN OVERWHELMING ENEMY.

Isn't this how most of us react to bad situations? When Satan throws one problem after the other at us, we become overwhelmed and sometimes feel hopeless and helpless as Gehazi did. We look at what we see in the physical and can see no deliverance. We begin to ponder and listen to the enemy's voice in our head that it will never be better and that we are doomed. This is how hopelessness sets in.

But Elisha did not see the situation in the natural. His spiritual eyes saw a very different picture. His reaction was simple, "Do not fear, for those who are with us are more than those who are with them." And Elisha said, "Lord, I pray, open his eyes that he may see."

I'm always blown away at the faith Elisha showed because the Word doesn't even say that he walked outside; he just spoke hope and truth to Gehazi, and then prayed for Gehazi to see through spiritual eyes as he did. But, after all, Elisha was a prophet.

And what did Elisha see in *the very same situation?* He saw deliverance; he saw hope. And, he wanted Gehazi to see what he saw! And what did he see? "The mountain was full of horses and chariots of fire all around Elisha." God's protection was there, even though it could not be seen with the natural eye. Then, Elisha prayed that the enemy forces would be struck with blindness, and they were.

It doesn't go unnoticed that the angelic forces of chariots of fire never actually acted on Elisha's behalf. But they were there protecting him. No doubt, if Elisha had asked the Lord for destruction of his enemies, it would have happened. God had proved his protection over Elisha and his ministry earlier when young men were ridiculing and reviling him and two bears had come and attacked them. What a story! However, I believe that God's heart, therefore, Elisha's heart, was to show mercy that day. Instead of killing his enemies, he chose life for them, even preparing a feast before sending them on their way.

This is how the Father wants *us* to react in life's situations. When we are in the midst of trouble, He wants us to pray, to stand on what we KNOW IS TRUTH: that God is GOOD, that He loves us, that He desires to give good gifts to His children, that He is working all things together for our good, that He is purifying us and refining us, that He WILL DELIVER us from the fire in His perfect way! He wants us to speak the Word and deliverance, because "life and death is in the power of the tongue and they that love it will eat its fruit" (Proverbs 18:21).

One of my most hopeless moments came many years ago when my husband and I were about to separate. I was so distraught over the impending separation, and kept believing that a miracle would happen to stop it, but it had not. On that particular day, I had turned in my two week notice at my job and the reality that my marriage seemed to be over hit me hard. It was very late at night and my husband and three young sons were all asleep. I was walking the floor weeping uncontrollably, and feeling more hopeless by the moment. I finally sat down on my couch and picked up my Bible and began to read. After a while, I laid it down, and in my total despair, cried out to the Lord: "Lord, Your Word says You have a peace that passes all understanding. If you do, please give it to me now."

IMMEDIATELY, I felt what can only be described as warm oil being poured on my head and, within seconds, it touched my toes! I took a deep breath, and my sobs ceased. My tears were gone! The total hopelessness I had experienced only moments before was also gone, replaced with the sweetest peace I had ever known. I gave many thanks to my Father for helping me, and then went and lay down and went straight to sleep!

How do I explain this? I'll tell you what I know: that He made a promise, that I as His born-again child asked for Him to show Himself strong for me, and that He did!

Like Gehazi, I had felt desperation, seeing no way out of my hopeless situation. But, in the end, like Elisha, I prayed, and the Lord answered me and delivered me.

Did the separation happen? It did, and lasted for a year. There were times I thought reconciliation would never take place, because a year is a long time. God was at work in both of our lives during that year, even though I had no idea how it would all end. But, I never again felt the hopelessness of that terrible night because I had come to know as a young believer that God is NOT a man that He could lie, and that His Word is true and His promises are real! I learned to trust Him, day by day, ending each night on my knees in prayer, and then falling fast asleep as I rested in Him.

It is so easy for us to think that God is not doing anything for us just because we can't see it. What do we say? "Lord, I've been praying for this situation forever and nothing is happening to change it!" If we could see in the spirit realm, it would astound us what God is doing! The Word shows us in Daniel 10 that there is indeed a battle in the heavenly realm between God's angels and demonic forces. From the first day that Daniel began to set his heart to understand, and to humble himself before his God, his words were heard, and an angel of God was sent to his defense. But for twenty-one days, there was a heavenly battle between the angelic and demonic forces which detained him. This is another glimpse into the spirit realm where there is always an unseen battle.

Our Lord is always fighting on our behalf. And, He is going to act in the way HE knows is for our best. We need only to trust Him! I pray you believe it, because it is truth!

Remember this: Gehazi saw his situation through the eyes of his FLESH and FEAR. Elisha saw the very same situation though the eyes of his GOD and FAITH. We, who know Him as Lord and Savior, have the ability to see life as Elisha did. May we choose daily to walk that out, for His Glory, knowing we will one day see face-to-face, as He has promised!

10 – HAVING A MERRY HEART

Proverbs 15:15—"All the days of the afflicted are evil, but he who is of a merry heart has a continual feast."

One morning, I was having my quiet time and I came across this wonderful verse that spoke to my heart so deeply. How many times had I read it before, I wondered? Because, this time, it stopped me with its rich beauty.

I immediately thought of the other verse in Proverbs 17:22: "A merry heart does good like medicine, but a broken spirit dries the bones."

As a side note, we need to remember who wrote Proverbs. Do you know? It was Solomon, King David's son with Bathsheba. God asked him what he would like Him to do for him when he became king after his dad, and his wonderful reply was that he would like wisdom to rule over his people. God was so pleased with his answer that He told him He would give him that wisdom, as well as riches and honor. So, we know that the words of the wisest man that ever lived are true and worthy of study!

It's really important that we know that even in the midst of much sorrow, we can still have an incredible, divine peace. We can have a merry heart and a continual feast.

So, let's break this verse down starting with what *affliction* means. It's defined as severe pain and suffering, disease, agony, mental or physical. So, affliction is **extreme** suffering. Mostly things *out* of our control.

What about a *merry heart*? That's *in* our control. Do you know the definition of *merry*? It means joyful, uninhibited enjoyment, festivity, delightful pleasure. So, the words *merry* and *feast* are intertwined. That's interesting.

And what about a *feast*? We don't have feasts like in Bible times. The Israelites had appointed feast times to celebrate and remember what God had done for them in the past to deliver them from being slaves in Egypt. There were seven feasts that they celebrated each year. Why? God did not want them to forget what He had done in the past; He wanted them to always remember His deliverance and provision. So, *feast* actually means to celebrate, a time of joy and abundance.

Think about what Solomon was saying in our terms: even if you must endure much severe suffering, you can have untouched enjoyment and celebration, if you have a merry heart.

Now, the last question that remains is how we can truly have a merry heart, a continual feast.

Well, there are many temporary givers of merriment, but only ONE permanent way we can have a nonstop feast in our heart, and that's from the only giver of real, true joy—Jesus.

You see, a merry heart is between you and Jesus alone. No one else can touch what goes on in your heart and Jesus' heart because that's on the inside. No one can touch your heart, period, unless you give them permission. The only one that can touch my heart is the person I give my heart to, which is a good reason to *never* give our heart away to the wrong person.

Jesus must be first. If you want a merry heart, you MUST have quiet time daily with Him. Satan is attacking you and your family DAILY whether you see it or not. Just as the Holy Spirit is always at work, so is Satan. God told us that Satan is a roaring lion, seeking who he may destroy (1 Peter 5:8). That's telling us that he is our very real enemy.

I look at people going through life, just living their life, without a relationship with Jesus. Everything looks great and they are just living life large. Then, one day, they receive news of a terrible attack on them or their family.

I have heard so many parents say, "I did not raise my child this way. The choices they have made are not what I taught them." And, here's what I always wonder: Did you teach your child to love Jesus and have a relationship with Him? All of us made bad choices growing up; that happens. I know I did. But, if we don't teach our children to love and serve Him by OUR example of putting Him first, we will one day pay the price in our families.

So, back to the merry heart! How does a merry heart give us a continual feast no matter what we are going through? Very simple. The Holy Spirit, Who lives within us, gives us the love of Jesus, the comfort of Jesus, the hope of Jesus, the joy of Jesus, the peace of Jesus, as He rules and reigns inside our hearts. Affliction hits, but *it* doesn't rule.

And, let's take it a step further: What about the effect on others of our merry heart and our continual feast? Having a merry heart is not just for us. It's for other people, too.

People don't have to be around us for long before they know what's going on inside our heart, do they? There's no mistaking the difference Jesus makes in our life. Remember Moses coming down from the mountain after having spent time with God getting the Ten Commandments? His countenance was so bright the people could not even look at him (Exodus 4:29–30). It was clear Who he had been with!

And, while I was studying this, the Lord reminded me again of something I don't want you to miss: This is beautiful and I love it. In the Old Testament, no one could look directly at God and live. Only the high priest could go into the Holy of Holies where the Ark of the Covenant sat, and only once a year (Hebrews 9:7). You just couldn't get too close and were commanded not to.

But, in the New Testament, the new covenant with Jesus, we are commanded to fix our gaze on Jesus, to seek Him with all our hearts, to get as close to Him as we can (Hebrews 12:2). As we do, we become like Him, and our countenances too will reflect His love and His presence which DRAWS OTHERS TO US AND THEN TO Him. Because it's just not normal to have a continual feast, especially in the midst of sorrow.

Remember the veil that separated the Holy of Holies' room from the outer court in the Temple? That veil was torn the second Jesus breathed His last breath! Why? What was God saying? God made sure everyone knew that the death of His Son opened the door to directly access Him. No more priests. Just JESUS!

So, we are without excuse. As we make time for everything in our life but Him, we are without excuse. In Revelation 3:20, Jesus said, "I stand at the door and knock: if any man hear My voice and open the door, I will come in to him, and will fellowship with him, and he with Me."

He is there knocking on the door of our hearts wanting to fellowship with us, wanting to have a continual feast with us.

I encounter people who clearly have that continual feast. I have a friend who was telling me a story recently. She was about to take a job with the government and had to have her picture taken. The photographer actually told her she couldn't smile because it's required to be somber in their ID picture. So, she said okay, trying not to smile. The photographer said, "You're still smiling." She said, "No, I'm not." And, the photograpHer said, "Yes, you are." After going back and forth, the photographer finally just took her picture. She said the outcome was a crazy expression and an unnatural, contorted face!

This friend loves the Lord, spends much time in His Presence, and her default is always a smile. We laughed together that, no matter how hard she tried, she just couldn't seem to erase the joy of the Lord that's always on her face. I just love that!

The apostle Paul said this in 2 Corinthians 4:7: "We have this light shining in our hearts, but we ourselves are like fragile clay jars containing this great treasure. This makes it clear that our great power is from God, not from us. We are pressed on every side by troubles, but we are not crushed. We are perplexed (uncertain), but not driven to despair, we are struck down but not destroyed. Through suffering, our bodies continue to share in the death of Jesus so that the life of Jesus may also be seen in us."

As you see, Paul didn't diminish the fact that he walked in much severe affliction. But, Paul had found the Source of a continual feast, and he held fast to that Source until he took his last breath.

There's a television pastor who says this: "I have an obligation to maintain a merry heart." He so wants others to know that Jesus can give us joy, merriment, and a continual feast by the Holy Spirit Who lives within us. No matter what. And He surely can!

I pray if you have not, that you will choose to enter into that continual feast with the Savior. Only He can help us look past and rise above our present, temporary circumstances and sorrows to the Hope of Glory we will one day enjoy for eternity with Him!

11 – OUR REFUGE AND OUR STRENGTH

Psalm 46:1–2—God is our refuge and strength, A very present help in trouble. Therefore, we will not fear, Even though the earth be removed, And though the mountains be carried into the midst of the sea.

Have you ever been really afraid? Has your world ever fallen apart and you had no idea how to fix it, no idea where deliverance could come from?

I know I have. And, I discovered through the love and mercy of the Father that He alone was my refuge, that He alone was my strength.

But, before I share my story, let's explore these two beautiful verses of promise. And, let's put it into words that are easier to understand. I'd say it like this: Because Jesus is my Savior, I don't have to be afraid, even in extreme circumstances.

And, let's break it down even further by looking at the actual meanings of the words in these verses. *Refuge* is a condition of being safe or sheltered from pursuit or danger, being protected; a recourse in difficulty, a retreat, a safe harbor, a sanctuary. It's a place where I can run to be safe from harm.

It makes me think of the word *refugee* that we hear so often today. A *refugee* is one who leaves a place of danger to find a place of safety. So, that means we are all refugees when we decide to leave the pull of the flesh and run to Jesus Who is our refuge.

One of my favorite Bible stories about a refugee is the story of Ruth and Naomi. Their family was forced to leave Bethlehem because of a severe famine and go to the country of Moab, Ruth's home country. While there, Naomi lost her husband and both of her sons. So, when the famine was over, she decided to go back home. Ruth refused to leave her side and both women returned to Bethlehem. Naomi was so broken that she told the women of Bethlehem not to call her Naomi, but to call her *Mara*, which meant bitter. But, because both Ruth and Naomi belonged to the Lord God, He had not abandoned them but had a great plan for their future. Could they even have conceived that Ruth would one day be a descendant of the Savior? God brought into the picture Boaz, who rescued them from poverty, and even gave Naomi a grandchild to care for. The story is a beautiful picture of God being their refuge through Boaz.

What is the meaning of *strength*? It's the quality of being strong, of being capable of withstanding great pressure or force.

I think of Queen Esther when I think of one who was given His great strength in a crucial time of need. She was in a situation where not only was her life in danger, but the lives of every single Jew in her land. And, as you know the story, she fasted for three days before going into the king's presence without being called, which could have meant death. And yet she did. Esther's bravery and courage saved the lives of her people as she was made to realize it was "for such a time as this" that she had been elevated to a position of royalty. God had placed her there and given her the strength and courage she needed.

Now, let's look at the last phrase of that first verse: "God is a very present help in times of trouble." We must take note that it says *in trouble*, not *from trouble*. There are surely times God rescues us from trouble but, very often, He is our help in the midst of trouble. As He was with Ruth and Naomi. As He was with Queen Esther.

And, since I believe every single word in the Bible is there for a reason, let's explore the meaning of *very, present,* and *help.*

Very means to a high degree, exceedingly, extreme, complete.

Present means without delay, immediate, existing now.

Help means to rescue, to save.

So, think about that awesome promise: He is there to rescue us without delay, in an extreme, complete way. It means He will rescue us one way or the other: by removing the situation, or by carrying us through it.

There are so many wonderful stories of God rescuing His own in the Bible. God rescued Noah and his family from the Flood. God rescued Daniel from the lions. God rescued Shadrach, Meshach, and Abednego from the fire. In each of those situations, God did not remove the trouble but showed Himself strong and carried them through the trouble to the other side. He rescued them all in His perfect way.

I love the story in Acts 12 of the Lord rescuing Peter from prison. King Herod had killed the disciple James, the brother of John, and had imprisoned Peter, intending to kill him after the feast days were over. But, an angel of the Lord was sent to rescue him in the middle of the night. His chains fell off and the angel led him safely out of the city.

And, then, in Acts 16, Paul and Silas were beaten and imprisoned by the Romans. At midnight, they were "praying and singing hymns to God" when He sent an earthquake to shake the prison foundations and loosen all their chains. This story is especially precious because they were unshaken by their trouble. The God they served was their everything, and their confidence in Him was clear to those around them. The jailer and all his family were saved that night because he witnessed their faith and the power of almighty God for His own!

In each of these stories of intense suffering and deliverance, we see that their lives could not be taken until the Lord said so.

Why? Because they all belonged to Him, and their end was in HIS hands.

I remember when I was younger and believed that obedience to the Father always meant immediate, visible rescue. I thought, if I just obeyed His voice, that everything would be rosy. I had fasted and prayed and obeyed the Lord in a really tough situation and, instead of things getting better, they had gotten worse. Much worse.

I was driving down the road that day, questioning the Father as to why my obedience had resulted in such suffering. I was asking Him why He had not rescued and delivered me from the terrible situation I was in.

And it was at that moment that one of the greatest miracles of my life happened.

In my peripheral vision, I saw a tiny window of Heaven open and heard a conversation between the Father and the Son. The Son said, "Father, she doesn't understand." And the Father said, "No, but she loves Me." And the window closed.

I was in total disbelief! I could not fathom what had just happened!

I broke down and wept in deep sobs repenting for questioning Him. And I KNEW, at that moment, that I didn't have to understand; I simply had to believe that He was my refuge and strength, that He would rescue me, and that I must trust Him to carry me through as I waited. And I had to learn that obedience is a must, regardless of the outcome. His ways are higher than our ways, we are told, and we cannot always understand His purpose.

The Lord directed me shortly after that to study the life of the apostle Paul. From the day the Lord appeared to Paul on the road to Damascus, he was never the same. He obeyed the Holy Spirit's voice from that day on, but suffered horribly in many ways. And look at how the Lord used his obedience: Paul wrote a large portion of the New Testament! The Lord gave Paul wisdom and knowledge and understanding and insight into the treasures of the Gospel and of Heaven. God was able to use Paul mightily just because of his obedience! And, no matter how severe Paul's suffering, God gave him an incredible strength to serve Him, and always rescued him until it was his time to die.

And, just as the Lord was always near Paul, He was with me in my situation; He carried me through to the other side. He simply had to teach me that obedience does not always result in immediate deliverance from suffering. But it can and should result in immediate peace. And even joy! "Joyful are those who obey His laws and search for Him with all their hearts." (Psalm 119:1)

Finally, there is much to be learned from the story found in Judges 20. The army of Israel was about to go to war against the tribe of Benjamin. There were "perverted men" in the ranks of Benjamin who had murdered the concubine of a Levite. The army of Israel demanded that the men be turned over to them for justice, but the Benjamites refused, resulting in a battle between them.

As they faced one another, they asked the Lord which tribe should go out to battle first and the Lord said, "Judah first." So, Judah went out to battle, but the army of Benjamin cut down 22,000 of them. The Israelites wept before the Lord and again asked counsel from Him. And the Lord told them to go up against them again.

So, on the second day, they obeyed and, this time, 18,000 of the Israelites were killed. This time, the Israelites went to the house of God and wept and fasted all day until evening, and then offered burnt offerings to the Lord. Once more, they inquired of the Lord and, this time, He said, "Go up, for tomorrow I will deliver them into your hand." And, this time, He did.

Here's what struck me about this story: The Israelites didn't question the Lord as to why they didn't have victory in the first or second battle. Instead of getting angry and questioning and turning away and saying that the Lord was not helping them, they ran straight back to Him each time, asking for guidance.

How pleased the Lord must have been that they wanted to obey Him, even after losing so many of their brethren! The Lord was still their source, their refuge and strength and help, their ONLY path to victory!

Let's end with the promise of the second verse where we began, and that is that we do not have to be afraid, "even though the earth be removed and the mountains cast into the sea." The Word has told us that the end times will bring much chaos and destruction. We have been informed that the days will be harsh. But . . . BECAUSE God is our refuge and strength, BECAUSE God is our very present help in trouble, we do not have to be afraid. We must always remember how He has shown Himself strong for us in the past, and know and believe and stand on the promise that He will do it again. He WILL rescue us!

In His perfect way. In His perfect time.

12 – THE DIFFERENCE A DAY CAN MAKE

Lamentations 3:22–23—Through the Lord's mercies we are not consumed, because His compassions fail not. They are new every morning; great is Your faithfulness.

Sometimes it's really hard to see past all the negative things going on in our lives and in the world, isn't it? And the unknowns. Especially the unknowns. Sometimes, the weight of it all can blind us to all the good things that are present in the here and now and the good things that may be coming, just around the corner.

That's when we, who know Jesus as Savior, need to do as David did when all seemed lost: encourage ourselves in the Lord. (1 Samuel 30) To remind ourselves of what the Lord has already done. The best way to do that is to look to the awesome stories of deliverance in the Word. And, for this chapter, the ones where just one day turned their whole lives around for good!

In 1 Samuel 30, we find a story of RESTORATION, full and complete. King David and his men had just returned from a victorious battle. I'm sure they were elated to return home to their families. But, when they got to Ziklag, they found to their horror that their wives and children and all possessions had been taken. The Word says that they all cried until they had no tears left. As we all would. And David's men were so distraught that they spoke of stoning him, blaming him for what had happened. So, what do you think David did at that point? "David encouraged himself in the Lord." Wow. And then, he sought the Lord for how to proceed. He then told his men to get ready, that they would pursue, overtake, and bring their families home. And that's exactly what happened. They went from losing everything to gaining everything. ALL was restored!

Another of my favorite stories is a story of HEALING. Remember the woman with the flow of blood found in Mark 5? This precious woman had suffered for twelve long years and had spent all she had at the hands of doctors, to no avail. They had only increased her pain. After so many years of suffering and exhausting every physical attempt for healing, most people would have given up. A flow of blood would most surely have made her constantly weak and in terrible pain. When Jesus passed through her town that day, hope must have risen in her heart from all the stories she had heard of His ability to heal. All she had left was this: a will to be healed and an incredible faith, which led her to press in to Jesus and touch the hem of his garment. And that was enough! The Word tells us that IMMEDIATELY the blood dried up and she was healed!

How about a story of DELIVERANCE? This one is found in 2 Chronicles 20, and it's the story of King Jehoshaphat of Judah. They were totally outnumbered as forces of their enemies had united and were en route to destroy them. When Jehoshaphat was told of their impending doom, he could have given up and fallen into despair. But instead, he "set himself to seek the Lord and proclaimed a fast throughout all Judah." And all the cities of Judah came together to jointly seek Him! The king stood in their midst and praised God for His great and mighty power, reminding everyone of how the Lord had shown Himself strong in the past and said, "We don't know what to do, but our eyes are upon You." Wow. I can't imagine anything that could have pleased God more than "only You can save us."

And, guess what happened? God spoke immediately through the prophet Jahaziel and told them not to be afraid, because the battle was His, not theirs. And this thought popped in my mind: The battle was God's because they GAVE IT TO HIM. It was God's because they acknowledged they could not fight and win on their own; they knew HE alone could bring them victory! And did He ever bring them victory! The next morning, they all rose early, set themselves in ranks with the singers and musicians first, and began marching TOWARD the enemy, as God had commanded. And, guess what they began to sing? "Praise the Lord, for His mercy endures forever." (Don't you just LOVE it?) So, the enemy began attacking each other until all were dead. And the spoil of jewelry and valuables on the fallen enemy took them three days to gather! Now, that's deliverance!

And, then there's our own story of PROVISION. Many years ago, our church felt called to begin a weekend backpack food ministry for children in our local schools. We were a small body of believers, but we knew that the Lord would provide if we would just step out in faith and commit to feeding the children in need. The numbers of needed bags continued to grow, until we became concerned as to how the financial need would be met. One day, I received a phone call from one of our members that he had something to bring me. He had received an insurance settlement and wanted to bring me a check because I was the treasurer. I was shocked when I opened that envelope. The check was almost $18,000, enough to cover food costs for over a year!

But, the most important story of the difference a day can make is the RESURRECTION story of our Lord Jesus. There is no greater difference than death to life! The disciples had lost their Master and Teacher and were hiding in fear and devastation. It's hard to imagine the things they were feeling: How could the Son of God die? How could evil have won? Why did He spend three years teaching them and loving them just to leave them alone? They had left their families, they had left all, to be with Him and this is how it would end? I'm sure they were heartbroken and confused, ready to go back to their former lives when the danger was past, if it ever could be past. And then that third day came! And the women came running to them telling them the Master was no longer in that grave but was risen! They saw Jesus die and now He lived again! How could it be? The change in the disciples from Jesus' death to His resurrection is one of the reasons we KNOW He lives. They went from hiding to going into "all the world and making disciples of all men" just as He commanded them to. Only seeing the RISEN Lord could have brought about such a change.

We serve a living God Who overcame death and the grave, just as He said He would!

We who know Him as Lord cannot afford to live out our lives in fear, in anxiety, in chaos. When the cares of this world try to knock us down and keep us down and overwhelm us, we must remind ourselves of Who we serve and the power of His great and mighty love toward us who believe. Here's a Scripture we need to keep in front of us at all times:

Ephesians 1:18–20—I pray that the eyes of your heart may be enlightened in order that you may know the hope to which He has called you, the riches of His glorious inheritance in His holy people, and His incomparably **great power for us who believe**. That power is the same as the mighty strength He exerted when He raised Christ from the dead and seated Him at His right hand in the heavenly realms."

What? Do you realize that He is saying His power toward us is the same as the power that raised our Lord Jesus from the dead? Do we walk in that knowledge? Do we believe that? As born-again children of the Most High God, we MUST believe!

There will always be stories of healing, of deliverance, of restoration, and of provision that we can look back on and REMEMBER. We must remember how He has shown Himself strong for others and for us in the past, and see how victory came.

David went straight to his source, the God he served, and found RESTORATION.

The woman with the flow of blood PRESSED IN AND BELIEVED THAT HE WAS HER SOURCE OF HEALING and He was.

King Jehoshaphat immediately called on the Name of the Lord and commanded all of his kingdom to do the same, and found DELIVERANCE.

The key is pressing in! The key is running to Him for help! The key is keeping our eyes on Him at all times, and when trouble comes, look unto HIM for help.

He alone is our Restorer, our Healer, our Deliverer, and our Provider! Is He that for you today?

13 – WORDS

Ephesians 4:29—Do not let any unwholesome talk come out of your mouths, but only what is helpful for building others up according to their needs, that it may benefit those who listen.

I was on my way to church one morning listening to the radio when I first heard the song "Mean Girls." A young girl had called into K-love to request the song and told the DJ that she loved the song because she so related to it. She knew the power of the hurt of words. She was eleven.

My heart hurt for such a young child, knowing she had been harmed by the words of her peers. My mind went back to my teenage years, when I had received the same wounds.

When I was fourteen, we moved to a new town called Ramer. I was immediately accepted by those sweet kids. They were an ideal group of young people who just seemed to love everybody. I was actually voted in by my friends as a cheerleader, and got class favorite, my greatest honor of all. Those were the best two years of my school experience and I still love those people today. Fifty years later.

But then, after two years, my Daddy got sick and had to retire. Which meant another move, this time to the big city of Montgomery. I was in a class of 1,500 students, in a school of over 4,000, and I felt totally lost. I made few friends because I was very shy and sad about leaving the friends I had left behind. I had to walk to school every day and would leave home as late as possible to avoid the isolation and loneliness I encountered once

I got there. The worst part of my day was lunchtime, because there were no assigned seats. Everyone could sit wherever they wanted. That meant I had to sit all alone at a table that held eight. In a lunchroom that held hundreds. All around me, the kids were laughing and having fun while I tried to look busy reading.

As I shared in a previous chapter, I had attended a revival at our church and, for the first time in my life, I had felt the nudging of the Holy Spirit. By the time the pastor gave the altar call, I was undone and went down to give my life to Jesus. Even though I was a preacher's daughter, church was more my life and what we did. But this was different and I knew what was happening. I could not have stayed in my seat, the call was so real.

From that time on, I tried to serve the Lord as best I knew how. I joined a group called Young Life, which definitely helped me.

Back then, people used to wear buttons that said things like "God Is Love" or "Jesus Loves You." They were large like political buttons. One I wore said "Jesus Is Like A Bridge Over Troubled Water." It was bright yellow and I loved it, because it made reference to a popular song of the day. I wore my buttons to school as a witness.

Back to that lunchroom where I sat at a table alone. One day, a girl from one of the popular tables walked over to me as the others at the table watched. She had never spoken to me before, so I wondered what her purpose was. She asked me, "How is Jesus like a bridge over troubled water?" I'm not sure what I said, but I responded. She nodded her head and turned around and walked back to her table as they all erupted in laughter. That was my first experience with a "mean girl."

I was so embarrassed and hurt. I had never been publicly ridiculed before, and I hated how it made me feel. But, even at that young age of sixteen, I realized I had suffered in a small way for my Jesus and accepted it as that. And, even though it no longer causes me pain today, I've never forgotten it.

So, as you see, I had the unique experience in my youth of knowing what it is to be popular, as well as knowing what it is to be unpopular and alone. And, as an adult, I am actually thankful for knowing both situations. I always taught my boys to take up for the underdog because there was a time that underdog was their Mama! I later learned that the apostle Paul actually wrote about knowing extremes in this life. Of knowing how to be full and how to be hungry, etc. (Philippians 4:11–13)

Why are children so cruel with their words to one another? Have they not been taught better? Or, is it the selfishness of youth?

Words have the potential to bless and to curse. Words can cut to our hearts or words can bless our hearts.

Are we teaching our children to be kind? Are we telling them the importance of building others up instead of tearing them down? Or, are we telling them to repay mean words with more mean words?

The Book of James talks extensively about our words. He refers to the *tongue* as "a fire, a world of evil among the parts of the body. It corrupts the whole body, sets the whole course of one's life on fire, and is itself set on fire by hell. It is a restless evil, full of deadly poison." (James 3:6) Strong words, but we all know they are true. And, once words are spoken, they cannot be retracted. We can apologize, even with tears, but our words remain.

This chapter is SO important to me because I want parents to teach their children kindness through their example. Kids will not do what you tell them to; they will do what you do. That living example is what they will one day follow, not your instruction.

But, it doesn't stop there. We must also follow Scripture when it tells us to teach our children the Word: to talk to them in the morning, during the day, and in the evening (Deuteronomy 11:9). As we teach them Scripture and live it out before them, they *will* one day follow. We have that promise in Proverbs 22:6:

"Train up a child in the way he should go, and when he grows older, he will not depart from it."

All three of my boys were very young when I presented the Gospel to them, but they were old enough to understand. I told them simply that the Bible says we are all sinners, that Jesus came to die and rise again to offer us salvation and that, unless they accepted Him as Savior, they could not go to Heaven. My sweet boys each prayed for that the very nights I shared the Gospel with them!

If we can just convince our sons and daughters that once they are saved and begin their walk with the Savior, their value, their worth, their identity comes not from the words or actions of others, but from their relationship with Jesus, they can be secure in their identity. They are now a child of The King, a son or daughter of The Most High God, and need to understand that no words of destruction from others have to have any power over them.

It's a lesson I so wish I had learned early on, but did not. I was in my forties when I finally realized who I was in Christ. I am His above all else, and that realization gave me perfect self-esteem, great security, and worth that the words of other cannot destroy! In this case, we do not think "more highly of ourselves than we ought." (Romans 12:3) We can simply be secure in His love and begin to love Him and others with that beautiful love He sheds abroad in our hearts. (Romans 5:5)

The result of teaching our children their worth in Christ will be princes and princesses not of this world. They will understand that the world does not revolve around them to have their every whim granted, but their world revolves around the Savior and His perfect will for their lives.

And, as they live that out, you will not see "mean girls" or "mean boys" hurting others. You will see loving sons and daughters bringing God's love to others as they fulfill His purposes.

What more could a Christian parent want for their children? Not a thing!

14 – SPEAK LIFE!

**Proverbs 18:21—Life and death are in the power
of the tongue and they that love it will eat its
fruit.**

One day, I was in a local pharmacy and felt impressed to
tell the clerk who was checking me out just how awesome of an employee she was. I had thought it many
times before but, on that particular day, I believed I needed to
verbalize my thoughts.

So, I proceeded to tell the young woman that I had been a
business owner for a long time, and that she was exactly the kind
of employee I had always looked for, but that was a rare find. I
shared how her smile, her kindness, and her obvious work ethic
were so impressive and I just wanted her to know. She was almost moved to tears and told me that she was overwhelmed. And
that my words had made her day!

As I left the pharmacy, I was reminded of the verse above
from Proverbs where King Solomon imparted the importance of
what we speak.

Many years prior, one of my sisters-in-law had shared this
verse with me. I was young in the Lord at that time and am so
ashamed to say I somewhat scoffed at the words, in my mind. I
had heard others share that we were to "speak life" and I thought
it was silly. Because I had no idea that my words could actually
have an impact on my life. I didn't know God's Word, so I was
unaware that the verse even existed. Over the years, as I've read
the Word and walk daily with my Savior, I've grown to love this

verse. In fact, I've quoted it many times to others and to myself in my own need.

Throughout the New Testament, Jesus made it clear that our faith, our belief, is related to His actions on our behalf.

Although I've already mentioned this story in the chapter on "The Difference a Day Can Make," I must mention it again here. It is the story from Luke 8 of the woman with the issue of blood and is one of my many favorites. The Bible tells us she had spent all the money she had on physicians and twelve years had passed, to no avail. She *said* to herself, "If I can just touch the hem of His garment, I will be made whole." And, as we know the story, she DID touch His garment and she WAS made whole. Do you remember what Jesus said when He found her? "Your faith has made you whole."

Wow. The Son of the Living God said that her faith contributed to her healing.

I believe the Lord is so pleased when we speak His Word in faith! I love to pray, "Father, Your Word says . . ." before I make my petitions to Him.

Jesus often made reference to this concept. When He was in His hometown in Mark 6, the Bible says, "He could not do many miracles there because of their unbelief." When He was speaking to the church leader whose daughter was dying, He said, "If you believe, all things are possible" (Luke 8:50).

One of the saddest stories in the Old Testament is found in Numbers 13. The Father had brought the Israelites, whom He had rescued from Egypt, to the border of the Promised Land. He told Moses to pick one leader from each tribe to spy out the land that He was about to give them. After forty days, they returned with a great report of the prosperity of the land and stated that it was truly "flowing with milk and honey."

But then, they made the terrible mistake of *speaking* of their enemies what they had SEEN from the eyes of flesh, instead of speaking what they should have KNOWN in their hearts. Ten of the men said they were not able to go up against the people, because they were stronger than them. They said it was a "land that devours its inhabitants" and "there we saw giants; and we were like grasshoppers in our own sight." Only Joshua and Caleb spoke through the eyes of faith. They said, "Do not rebel against the Lord, nor fear the people of the land, for they are our bread; their protection has departed from them, and the Lord is with us."

Sadly, the people believed the report of the ten spies instead of Joshua and Caleb. They rebelled against God by *saying* the Lord had brought them into the wilderness to die; that it would be better to return to Egypt. They even said Joshua and Caleb should be stoned.

God was very angry with the Israelites because they had so quickly forgotten all the miracles He had done in their sight and on their behalf, proving He alone would be their Provider and their Rescuer. And here's the part that I want you to hear: In Numbers 14:28, the Lord said, "As I live, just as you have *spoken*, so I will do to you." They made the mistake of speaking death over themselves and rejecting God's promises for them. So, the ten spies died by the plague, and those who spoke death never made it to the Promised Land.

Do our words matter to the Lord? They most certainly do. Because our words are a reflection of our heart, of our faith, of our belief in the love and power of our precious God toward us.

Admittedly, there are times of weakness when our faith and our words falter. There are times when the attacks are so relentless that we want to give up.

I remember one night, shortly after the death of my Daddy, that I received two very bad reports within a time frame of less than an hour. I was so broken down and shaken that I began sobbing and saying to the Lord, "Please, let me die; please, just let me die." Those were the only words that I could speak in between the wrenching sobs. It was a terrible night. But I had once heard a

Bible teacher say, "If all you can do is cry, cry to Jesus." And that's what I did until the sobs ceased.

Thankfully, because He is the "lifter of my head" (Psalm 3:3), He spoke peace to His broken child and carried me through. Because that's what our Daddy God does for His children. And I'm so grateful He forgave me for speaking death when I repented.

So, let's look at Mark 9:24 and the story of the father whose son had a demon and would throw himself into the fire. When he asked Jesus to heal his son, Jesus asked him if he believed. He replied truthfully: "Lord, I believe. Help my unbelief!" I think this man knew that Jesus could see his heart: a heart that desperately wanted his son to be made whole and believed Jesus could accomplish that, but still had a measure of doubt.

That most certainly describes all of us at times. But Jesus, Who sees and knows all, took that measure of faith from that father and He healed his son. It was enough. I am so grateful for a Savior Who loves and forgives and blesses and heals even when our faith is weak.

Does the Father always give us what we pray for when we believe He will? Not always. But only because He knows what is best and He knows what we need more than we do. *And the perfect will of the Father always supersedes the will of the child.*

So, let's remember to speak life, even when, and especially when, we can't see a good end to a situation.

Let's stand on the promises of God.

And let's make Him smile as we speak His Words back to Him in faith by standing not on what we see, but on what we KNOW! And that is that God is good all the time. All the time!

15 – REPAY EVIL WITH GOOD

1 Peter 3:8–9—Finally, all of you be of one mind, having compassion for one another; love as brothers, be tenderhearted, be courteous; not returning evil for evil or reviling for reviling, but on the contrary blessing, knowing that you were called to this, that you may inherit a blessing.

How many of us will admit that no matter how long we've been saved, our first response to an evil act against us is to want to repay evil with evil? It's so hard to be kind when someone has treated us badly. But we've been instructed by our Savior through the disciple Peter to do just that.

What causes me the most grief is getting blindsided. If I'm expecting a possible verbal altercation, I don't normally get wounded. But, when I'm thinking all is well and I get hit with harsh words out of nowhere, I can get deeply hurt. And want to lash back.

I still remember an incident that took place at church. Yep, the wound of a brother. Well, it was a sister actually. I almost walked away from my church all because I was blindsided by a sister in the Lord. I was hurt and angry and began this conversation with the Lord from my pew: "I cannot believe how she just said that to me. How dare she talk to me that way? After all I've done here, and this is how I'm treated? When I walk out that door, I will NEVER return."

I'm so grateful the Lord didn't let me leave there with that same frame of mind!

The sermon that day was on the healing waters of the Jordan River. Remember the story of Naaman, a renowned captain of the Syrian army who went down into the Jordan River at the instructions of Elisha and was healed of leprosy? His heart was hard because he wanted Elisha to SPEAK healing over him; he didn't want to dip in a muddy river. But his servants made him realize his healing could only come from obedience, so he complied. And he was healed. The pastor closed the sermon that day and began the altar call, speaking directly to my need without any idea of what that sister had said to me. My hard heart had been "tenderized" by the Word and I went down for prayer. I laid my hurt and anger down and decided the answer was not to walk away, not to repay evil with evil.

Have you ever been in a similar situation? Probably so. And, like me, your reaction may have been to lash out or get angry and just decide to quit. I think that's normal.

But, it's not what Jesus told us to do. And, it's not what He did.

He didn't just tell us what to do; He showed us by His own actions that it's possible to repay evil with good.

Some may think it's a sign of weakness to overlook a wrong, to repay evil with good. But that's just not true. It takes a lot more resolve to let go of a wrong than to hold onto it. I know. I've done both. And, it's just so freeing to repay evil with good. The aggressor is usually shocked by your good response.

I currently work the front desk at a hotel. Most customers are very sweet but, on occasion, I've had customers walk in the door, rude and snappy. I remember one lady who was that way, and she had a cast on her arm. I overlooked her rudeness and responded by saying, "Bless your heart; how did you hurt your arm?" That simple comment and question of concern completely changed her attitude and we began a conversation.

Did that come from the goodness that just happens to be my natural response? Absolutely not! Because the normal flesh response would be to make her room key and get her out of the lobby as soon as possible. But the Holy Spirit has some beautiful fruits, one of which is kindness. And HE who lives in my heart gave me the words to show the customer concern. HE knew she was hurting and needed a kind word. And, most importantly? My awesome Father God was glorified! That's what matters.

I always think about Joseph when repaying evil with good is discussed. As you will recall the Bible story, his brothers actually sold him into slavery when he was only seventeen, and told his father that he had been killed by a wild animal. Talk about cruel! All because they were jealous. Then, he was lied about by the wife of the man he worked for in Egypt and was thrown into prison because of it. Finally, at the age of thirty, he was given the divine meaning of the Pharaoh's dream and was elevated to second in the kingdom because of knowing the interpretation. And then? His brothers came to Egypt to buy grain during a famine. Joseph recognized them, but they did not recognize him.

Think of the power Joseph now had to get even with his brothers. They had robbed him of his home. They had robbed him of his father. They had ruined his life for a time. He could now have every one of them killed. But, instead, he showed them mercy. In the end, he wept and embraced them all and forgave them. He brought them all, including his father, to Egypt and gave them a home. And here's what he told them: "You meant evil against me, but God meant it for good, to bring it about that many people should be kept alive, as they are today. So do not fear; I will provide for you and your little ones." (Genesis 50:20–21)

Wow. The beauty of repaying evil with good! Joseph understood that vengeance belonged to God. And he repaid evil with forgiveness and kindness.

Why is it so important to repay evil with good? There are so many reasons. Our words have the ability to bless, and our words have the ability to curse and tear down. Proverbs 15:1 says, "A gentle response defuses anger, but a sharp tongue kindles a temper-fire." Truth! If we respond to evil with evil, it's like throwing fuel on the fire and really bad things can be said and done. Things that are very difficult to retract. And Proverbs 25:11 says that, "The right word at the time is like precious gold set in silver." A good, kind word in response to evil is definitely precious in the sight of God.

More importantly, our responses to evil can honor God, or can dishonor Him. Let it not be said of us that we have brought shame to His Name.

I once had a sister in the Lord betray a confidence of mine. It was a very serious betrayal that caused great hurt to numerous people. I was crushed, broken, and undone. And my first response was to call that sister and confront her. But the Holy Spirit very emphatically told me no. And He told me why. The harm was done. It could not be undone. And to confront this sister would have been throwing "fuel on the flame" and it would have gotten bigger and bigger and caused even more harm. Instead, I had to learn and move on. And let it go. And NOT repay evil with evil.

We must never forget there are two sides to this: There are those who hurt us and there are those we hurt as well. Sometimes, we just spurt out our thoughts because we've just GOT to speak our mind without regard to the wounds it may cause. But, just as we want mercy from others, we must grant mercy and choose to repay evil with good.

My prayer for all who read this today is that you can choose to be obedient and honor our precious Father God by repaying evil with good! Remember what He said, "It is to our Father's glory that we bear much fruit." May we all bear the fruit of the Holy Spirit each day: love, joy, peace, patience, kindness, faithfulness, gentleness, goodness, and self-control!

16 – JESUS, OUR PERFECT SHEPHERD

Psalm 23—The Lord is my shepherd; I shall not want. He makes me to lie down in green pastures; He leads me beside the still waters. He restores my soul. He leads me in the paths of righteousness for His name's sake. Yea, though I walk through the valley of the shadow of death, I will fear no evil, for You are with me. Your rod and Your staff, they comfort me. You prepare a table before me in the presence of my enemies; You anoint my head with oil; my cups runs over. Surely goodness and mercy shall follow me all the days of my life, and I will dwell in the house of the Lord forever.

If you were raised in church, you no doubt memorized Psalm 23. As a pastor's daughter who attended church three times a week, I remember being taught this verse at an early age. As a child, though, it was more of an accomplishment than being able to grasp the comfort and promises of these verses.

A few years ago, a friend shared a book with me about real-life shepherds. It was so insightful because it was written from the standpoint of one who had lived the life. Although I can't remember the name of the book, I still do remember many of the truths he shared. And I thought it would be great to take the

Psalm 23 and show the correlations between the life of an earthly shepherd and the life of the Good Shepherd.

"The Lord is my shepherd; I shall not want."

When a shepherd buys a sheep, he marks them as his own by a specific cut in their ears. From that point on, shepherds are responsible for caring for their sheep at every moment. Their every need is supplied by the shepherd.

How the Lord must love us to have called Himself a shepherd! Did you know that a shepherd was considered the lowliest profession of all, so low, in fact, that a shepherd could not testify in a court of law? His testimony was worthless. Our precious Savior took on the role of our Good Shepherd to care for His sheep and He calls us His own! When we become His, we are marked by the Cross of Christ! And He will supply our needs, according to His perfect will.

"He makes me to lie down in green pastures; He leads me beside the still waters. He restores my soul."

Shepherds must take the sheep out of the fold to lead them to green pastures for food and to lead them to water. But sheep are very skittish animals that scare easily. They will not even lie down unless they feel safe.

And, as sheep who belongs to the Good Shepherd, He gives us peace and calms our anxious hearts and gives us rest. He IS our peace.

"He leads me in the paths of righteousness for His name's sake."

Shepherds use their staff to keep sheep on the path of safety. They learn his voice as he teaches them to listen and obey.

Our Good Shepherd leads us through the voice of the Holy Spirit speaking to us saying, "This is the way; walk in it." (Isaiah 30:21) He also tells us in John 10:27 that His sheep know His voice, and He knows them and they follow Him.

"Yea, though I walk through the valley of the shadow of death, I will fear no evil, for You are with me. Your rod and Your staff, they comfort me."

Once shepherds take their sheep out of the fold, they must protect them from dangerous animals. The rod is used to beat a predator back and also to discipline a sheep who refuses to obey the shepherd. And, once out of the fold, the shepherd cannot leave the sheep for even a moment. They require more care than any other farm animal. If they are too far from the fold, the shepherd must spend the night in the elements with the sheep resulting in the shepherd smelling like the sheep he loves. The older sheep learn to stay beside the shepherd, but the younger ones are prone to wander. And, if a sheep falls over and has not been recently sheared, the weight of the wool keeps it from being able to stand. After a few hours in the sun, the sheep will die if the shepherd is not there to pick them up. I can only say wow to the correlations here!

Staying close to the Good Shepherd is our protection as well! He has promised never to leave us or forsake us. The enemy of our soul is that hungry lion, seeking to devour us! Just as the wild animals seek to destroy the sheep, so Satan comes to steal, kill, and destroy God's creations (John 10:10). And, just as young sheep are prone to wander, young Christians require discipleship and close connections to the Body of Christ to keep on the path of righteousness. And the weight of the wool? We, as sheep of the Good Shepherd, fall down on this road of righteousness, too. We need His tender and mighty Hand to pick us up and set us on our feet again and uphold us. And He most surely does.

"You prepare a table before me in the presence of my enemies; You anoint my head with oil; my cup runs over."

A good shepherd is ready to meet any need his sheep may have. He makes them feel safe and loved in his care. In this case, though, King David begins to speak of himself as a king instead of a sheep. He describes the care of the shepherd as being like a banquet prepared for him in his enemies' presence. He is being cared for and blessed in abundance and without fear.

We, who belong to Him, must realize our standing as children of the Most High. Being daughters and sons of the Most High God, brothers and sisters of the King of Kings, is a title that gives us a security and blessing like no other. We can live in peace and without fear as we stand on His promise to supply all of our needs, according to His riches in glory. (Philippians 4:19)

"Surely goodness and mercy will follow me all the days of my life and I will dwell in the house of the Lord forever."

He describes his future as one who will never have to worry again, but KNOWS that he is protected and destined to live with His Shepherd for eternity.

And this is the same promise for all of us who belong to Him!

Sadly, though, there are bad earthly shepherds who do not take proper care of their sheep and neglect them. Those sheep are thin, in danger, and afraid. In Jeremiah 23:1–6, Jesus spoke of bad spiritual shepherds who destroyed and scattered His sheep. He said they would be punished for their evil deeds, and that He would bring back His flock to His fold.

Jesus said in John 10:11 that He is a good shepherd and that a good shepherd lays down his life for the sheep. And that is exactly what He did for us.

I love the story Jesus told in Matthew 18 of the shepherd who had one hundred sheep, but one wandered from the fold. I love how he left the ninety-nine to go after the one and bring it back. All of His parables are beautiful pictures of life which make clear His love and purposes for us. In my backsliding days, I was that sheep who wandered away. I love to use the word *wooed* because that is what my Savior did to bring me back. He pursued my heart and made me realize He was the only One who could save me and give me peace. And, when I repented, He picked me up and brought me back to Him. I praise His Holy Name!

I read a true story about sheep that is a picture of the Body of Christ caring for one another. The sheep were in a fold, and one of the sheep was trying to escape through a break in the fence. But the other sheep sensed his disobedience and the danger that awaited him and actually got in his way and barred his ability to escape. The wayward sheep could not leave the pen because it was surrounded by the others.

Now, that story is nothing less than precious! It is straight from the Word, my friends! James 5:19–20 tells us this: "Brothers, if anyone among you strays from the truth, and anyone may turn him back, let him know that he who turned back a sinner from the straying of his way will save a soul from death, and will cover a multitude of sins." We sheep can help protect the Body of Christ, can be His Hands and Feet, by speaking truth and love to our brothers and sisters, our fellow sheep, when we see they are going astray.

I will tell you this: There is no one who knows us sheep better than the Shepherd! There is no one who knows our ways, our skittishness, our lack of wisdom, our proneness to wander from the safety of His arms, better than Him. And, who loves us, who wants to keep us safe and be our everything, more than the Shepherd? I can assure you the answer is no one!

So, stay close to the Shepherd! Listen to His voice and obey! Let Him lead you and guide you daily and one day take you to your eternal home!

17 – PUT ON THE GARMENT OF PRAISE

Isaiah 61:1–3—"The Spirit of the Lord God is upon Me, Because the Lord has anointed Me to preach good tidings to the poor; He has sent Me to heal the brokenhearted, to proclaim liberty to the captives, And the opening of the prison to those who are bound; to proclaim the acceptable year of the Lord, And the day of vengeance of our God; to comfort all who mourn, To console those who mourn in Zion, To give them beauty for ashes, The oil of joy for mourning, The garment of praise for the spirit of heaviness; That they may be called trees of righteousness, The planting of the Lord, that He may be glorified."

I'll never forget the day our youngest son, Brent, walked in the door and said these words: "The Lord is calling me to join the Army and be a chaplain so I can minister to soldiers." He was nineteen years old.

My twins had already married and left home. My Brian had stayed close but my Brandon had moved four hours away to be in ministry. We had helped him move and, when it came time to say goodbye, I thought my mama's heart would break in two. I think my goodbye lasted fifteen minutes. I just didn't think I could drive off without him! And, when we walked out the door and left him there, I was completely undone. If you're a mama you understand. Even though we let them go physically because we must, our hearts never let go.

I will never forget the feeling that overcame me the moment my babies were first laid in my arms. A love so deep, a new kind of love, completely overwhelmed me. I became an instant mama bear, willing to do anything to love and protect them. The truth is that the feeling of that love never changes, even though our relationship must, as they grow older. So deep inside where that mama's love lies, we hold on forever to that little one because completely letting go of them is just not possible. You look at my son and see a grown man. I look at my son and see that little boy who stole my heart the moment I laid eyes on him. That is my baby forever. That is how we feel.

And, now, my youngest son was not just about to leave home but to join the Army. I wouldn't even be able to talk to him for weeks. How could I bear it?

As thankful as you are when your child is serving the Lord and then goes on to fulfill their calling, joining the military, especially during wartime, is not what a mom wants to hear. I immediately began to explain all the reasons that was not a good idea. He had been diagnosed with ADD many years before, so that was my first line of defense. Hoping and praying he had heard wrong, I moved on.

It was not many weeks, however, until there was a knock at my front door, and there stood an Army recruiter. I have no doubt my expression relayed my dismay at his presence. He stayed a while, listened to and shot down my ADD reasoning (he was ADD, also, and the rigidity of their schedules had been perfect for him), and explained all the positives the Army would afford him. I was polite, but didn't think I'd make it until he left. I immediately went to my bedroom, shut the door, and cried my eyes out.

It was the first of many tears I would shed over this calling. I tried everything I could think of to stop him, but he would not be deterred. He went ahead and signed up. Over the course of the next few months, I prayed, cried, and grieved. I spent many days on my knees, crying out for my child. It was in this time that the Lord revealed a great truth to me that carried me then and continues to carry me seventeen years later.

Isaiah 61 tells us so many comforting reasons the Lord Jesus came to earth. One of those reasons is to bind up the broken-hearted. And one of the ways He would do that is through the garment of praise. As I knelt before Him in prayer, He combined three verses in my mind. Here's what He said, "I came to give you the garment of praise for the spirit of heaviness" (Isaiah 61:3), "As you praise Me, I inhabit the praises of my people" (Psalm 22:3), and "In My Presence is fullness of joy" (Psalm 16:11).

So, as I praised Him in my brokenness, He would come and bring fullness of joy. I was overwhelmed at this truth! Only He could have placed those three verses in my mind in that order to show me the power of His love! And so I began to praise Him through my tears that day, and I found He was right. His presence was truly with me, and I began to feel His joy in the midst of my worry and concern for my child.

One night, I lay in bed praying, unable to sleep. Here's what I heard and I *knew* it was the voice of the Holy Spirit: "I need a light in the darkness, and Brent is that light." Wow. So many emotions flooded over me. The Lord had made clear that this was His will, and even told me why. I was encouraged, albeit temporarily. Just being real.

As the day approached for his departure, I began to pray another prayer: "Lord, if there be any way and if this is not Your will, please stop him from leaving. (Does Moses come to mind? Or, maybe Gideon?) Let there be some mild medical reason, like a broken finger or toe. But, if not, I will know that I know this thing is from You."

I'm ashamed to say that although He had spoken to me so clearly, my mama's heart just kept questioning.

The day came and there was no broken limb. So I knew. I wish I could say that it was easy to let him go, but it was not. I can still cry over the memory today. But, what I can say is that the Lord was with my son and was with me. He carried me those four years and brought my child home from serving overseas.

As painful as letting him go was, I realized that the Lord had a plan and a purpose for us both. He had a great lesson to teach me, for sure. As my pastor son, Brian, says, "Nothing is wasted for a child of God."

I was and am so proud of my son for answering the call to serve! And I have never forgotten what the Lord taught me in the grief of letting him go. So many times in life, sadness and pain have tried to overtake me. But something truly miraculous happens when you begin to praise Jesus! Especially out loud! With a voice high and strong (Psalm 81:1)! I think our Father God is SO pleased with praise that He truly does inhabit our praises! And I believe and KNOW that, when He does, His joy is present and it overtakes us. Yes, I can testify to that truth!

One morning, I was feeling especially low when I got in my car headed to work. As usual, my radio was blaring (I like loud music!) from the day before. And, guess what song was playing? "It's a Good Morning" by Mandisa. Can you listen to that song and not praise the One Who can surely give us a good morning? So, as I drove that six minutes to work and sang along with her, my spirit lifted and I walked into my job lighthearted and with a good attitude that had completely turned around!

I'll say it like this: When we lift up the Name of Jesus, He lifts us up! Don't you love that?

On another occasion, I had gone to clean the church for someone. I decided to take advantage of listening to praise and worship music as I cleaned, knowing I would be alone and could sing as loud as I wanted! I put on a worship CD and the first song that came on was "Everlasting God." As I began to sing along and praise, the Presence of the Lord was so strong that I could not stand! I fell to my knees and worshipped, just me and My Savior, in that room! Talk about precious! It was so wonderful to experience His love and His power as I worshipped that Name above all Names! If you've never gotten alone to sing and praise the Lord God, my heart hurts for you! When you reach out your hands toward Heaven and praise that most beautiful, powerful Name, it can only uplift, heal, and take you to the Heavenly places with Him!

If we refuse to praise Him, we must remember Jesus Himself said that the rocks would have to cry out. (Luke 19:40) May we not be guilty of withholding praise from the One Who loves us more than we could ever imagine!

Here's what's so important for me to share: There is comfort, there is hope, there is even joy to be had in the midst of life's trials if we will fall on that Rock which is Jesus. He came to earth because of His great love for us. He died and rose again to make a way for us to come to the Father and be saved. And, He sent His Holy Spirit to live in our hearts to be our Helper, our Comforter, and our Teacher in all things.

My precious Daddy told me once that the hard times in life have the ability to break us or to make us. He said that we can be like glass that breaks and shatters from the blows, or we can be like steel that withstands it all. But, he made clear that **only** the power of Almighty God in the Name of Jesus makes that possible. I have found that to be absolute truth.

And, I will stand and testify that there is no comfort and no peace to be found that is greater than the divine peace that passes all understanding that He gives!

So, put on that garment of praise today: Turn on worship music, open that mouth, and sing and praise and even dance unto the Savior (like King David did), and give Him the unlimited glory He is so worthy of!

18 – VICTORY IN THE BATTLE AGAINST SATAN

Matthew 4:1–4—Then Jesus was led by the Spirit into the wilderness to be tempted by the devil. After fasting forty days and forty nights, He was hungry. The tempter came to him and said, "If You are the Son of God, tell these stones to become bread. Jesus answered, "It is written . . . ."

There is so much for us as believers to learn from this story about our Lord Jesus. Many questions arise as to why He had to suffer in the many ways He did. But, as we seek truth, we find truth, as the Holy Spirit leads us into ALL TRUTH.

And, here IS truth: We can fight this fight against Satan and win. We just have to know how! And Who was and is our forever model on how to be victorious? There is only One perfect model, and that is Jesus!

Let's start with the background of chapter 4. Jesus had not yet begun His earthly ministry. He had just been baptized by John and the Holy Spirit had descended upon Him in the form of a dove.

We are then told that Jesus was "led by the Spirit into the wilderness to be tempted by the devil." As I read and studied this, I asked the Father why. Why would our Lord Jesus, He who knew no sin, have to go through this? And His reply? For you, all for you, to show YOU how to be victorious against the enemy of your soul. How wonderful!

As a side note, but an important note, Jesus did something else precious just for us, just to show us how to live. He washed Judas' feet. Again, why? Jesus knew that Judas' soul was about to be lost for all eternity. One reason had to be that He did it because it was just Who He was and is; He is all love. But, another reason had to be showing us what unconditional love and forgiveness looks like. He washed Judas' feet for US. As an example for US.

Back to the story. Verse two then says that Jesus fasted for forty days and forty nights and afterward He was hungry. So, how did Satan choose to tempt Him first? In the area where he thought He might be weak.

This is exactly how Satan tempts us—in the area where he thinks we are weak. So, he said to Jesus, "If You are the Son of God, command that these stones become bread." And how did the Son of the Living God reply? "IT IS WRITTEN, 'Man shall not live by bread alone but by every word that proceeds from the mouth of God.'" He was quoting Deuteronomy 8:3. What was He telling Satan? Very simply this: I need physical food to feed my body, but I need God's Word more to feed my spirit. Satan had no reply.

Next, he took Jesus to Jerusalem, to the top of the Temple, and said to Him, "If you are the Son of God, throw Yourself down. For it is written (quoting Psalms), 'He shall give His angels charge over you,' and 'In their hands they shall bear you up, lest you dash your foot against a stone.'" (He was trying to entice Jesus to sin by questioning whether or not He was the Messiah and trying to get Him to prove it.) Again, our Lord replied, "IT IS WRITTEN, 'You shall not tempt the Lord your God.'" Notice here that Satan used Scripture to tempt Jesus to sin. Satan is a fallen angel and he knows the Word. Never, never, be so foolish to think that someone is real just because they quote Scripture. Matthew 7:15–17 SAYS BY THEIR (TRUE CHRISTIANS) FRUIT,

YOU SHALL KNOW THEM. Not by the words they speak. Not by how many Bible verses they can quote. Dear God, give us all wisdom, open our eyes to be able to discern who is real and who is not! We are too easily deceived!

Lastly, he took Jesus up on a mountain and showed Him the world and said, "All these things I will give You if You will fall down and worship me." This time, Jesus said to him, "Away with you, Satan! For IT IS WRITTEN, 'You shall worship the Lord your God and Him only you shall serve.'" And the devil left Him, and the angels came and ministered to Him.

So, what has the Lord just taught us in this story? HE HAS SHOWN US THAT WE FIGHT SATAN WITH THE WORD!

Ephesians 6:10 says this: "Be strong in the Lord and in the power of His might. Put on the whole armor of God that you may be able to stand against the schemes of the devil." There are many parts of the armor of God, but the one part that is called a weapon is the "sword of the Spirit which is the WORD OF GOD." This is exactly what Jesus did in this story: He used the sword of the Spirit to fight against Satan and win!

When I was in school, our teachers liked to get us to reword a sentence without changing its meaning. I would reword this verse this way: *If we DON'T put on the whole armor of God, we WON'T be able to stand against the schemes of the devil. We will be defeated if we don't prepare for battle. WHEN WE DON'T PUT ON THE WHOLE ARMOR OF GOD DAILY, WE WILL BE WEAK AND SUSCEPTIBLE.* Satan is described in the Word as a "roaring lion seeking whom he may destroy." And who do lions go after? The weak, the ones who wander from the flock.

Can you imagine a soldier going out to battle without his weapon and expect to win? We would say that is crazy and, yet, that is what we do every day that we don't put on the WHOLE ARMOR OF GOD. Soldiers in battle are told that they can never be without their weapon. It can never leave their side, even for a moment. Why? Because the enemy can strike at any time and they must be ready.

So, what is the whole armor of God? It's found in Ephesians 6:14–18. "Stand firm then, with the belt of truth buckled around your waist, with the breastplate of righteousness in place, and with your feet fitted with the readiness that comes from the gospel of peace . . . Take up the shield of faith, with which you can extinguish all the flaming arrows of the evil one. Take the helmet of salvation and the sword of the Spirit, which is the word of God."

Sometimes, it seems that our lives are so out of control, so out of order. It's like we are just floating along and hoping that things turn out okay, instead of following and obeying the Lord's commands. We must prepare for the battle of life. Like it or not, we are soldiers of the Cross; we are warriors in this battle for our soul, for the souls of our children, and for the souls of others; and, we cannot afford to waste time and walk in disobedience.

One morning, the Holy Spirit put these two words in my mind: *empowered* or *overpowered*. We are either empowered by the Holy Spirit as we put on the armor of God, or we will be overpowered by Satan.

I will share a personal story regarding this. One of my sons (when he was only five) began to fall under the direct attack of Satan. It began at his day care when he would lay down for a nap. He came home and told me that Satan was putting terrible thoughts in his mind and he was being tormented. When I asked him what was going through his mind, he would not say, only that it was horrible and that he couldn't make it go away. I was a young mother and a young believer, so I had no idea how to help my son. I told him to speak the Name of Jesus when it happened and he did, but said when he stopped, the thoughts returned. I was baffled; until one night, when we were reading his Bible, we came upon Matthew 4. The truth was revealed to me that night and, before he went to sleep, I taught him Scripture. The next day, he came home so happy and said that it worked—he spoke his Bible verse and Satan left him!

Think of this: Satan brings up your past in your mind, you respond with—IT IS WRITTEN, "IF ANY MAN BE IN CHRIST, HE IS A NEW CREATURE; OLD THINGS ARE PASSED AWAY, BEHOLD, ALL THINGS ARE BECOME NEW" (2 Corinthians 5:17), and "IF WE CONFESS OUR SINS, HE IS FAITHFUL AND JUST TO FORGIVE OUR SINS AND CLEANSE US FROM ALL UNRIGHTEOUSNESS" (2 John 1:9).

Satan brings up your problem with finances and tells you that you are a failure, and you respond with—IT IS WRITTEN, "THE RIGHTEOUS HAVE NEVER BEEN FORSAKEN OR THEIR CHILDREN BEGGING FOR BREAD" (Psalm 37:25), and "HE WILL SUPPLY ALL OF MY NEEDS ACCORDING TO HIS RICHES IN GLORY" (Philippians 4:19), and SEEK YE FIRST THE KINGDOM OF GOD AND HIS RIGHTEOUSNESS AND ALL THESE THINGS WILL BE ADDED TO YOU (Matthew 6:33).

Whatever Satan attacks you with there is Scripture to counteract that lie. Satan is a liar and the father of all lies (John 8:44). And, the Word says that God is not a man that He could lie (Numbers 23:19), and that the Holy Spirit will bring us into all truth (John 16:13).

You can't use the sword of the Spirit, the Word of God, if you don't KNOW THE WORD. Jesus didn't have time to go look up a verse when Satan came against Him. As the Author of the Word, He had the Word in His heart and was ready to use that weapon against Satan. This is truth: The more Scripture you learn and take to heart, the more you get to know the Lord and the more you will love Him! And the more you will be ready to take on the attacks of your adversary.

Read the Word. Know the Word. Fight with the Word. And you WILL be victorious!

19 – WHAT'S THE STATUS OF YOUR HARVEST?

Galatians 6:9—And let us not grow weary while doing good, for in due season we shall reap if we do not lose heart.

Talk about a verse that's packed full of real-life instruction, but this is it!

Where do you find yourself in your calling? Are you full of fire and hope and daily driven to accomplish the Lord's purpose in your life? Are you getting discouraged at all the knocks and blows that have come your way? Or are you almost ready to pack it in and give up?

The Word makes it plain that there will be times we will fall. "The steps of a good man are ordered by the Lord, And He delights in his way. Though he fall, he shall not be utterly cast down, for the Lord upholds him with His hand." (Psalm 37:23–24)

I personally know how rough the road of righteousness can be sometimes. I know how hard it is to keep going in the face of adversity and at times, hopelessness. I know how it sometimes seems we are being tested and tried. Or maybe even being punished. But I have learned the secret of holding fast and determining to never stop His call on my life.

Have you ever had a vegetable garden? I've had a garden twice in my life. The first time it was massive. I was trying to grow cucumbers, squash, okra, peas, butterbeans and tomatoes, all my very favorite vegetables! A friend had tilled the ground for me and got it all ready for planting. I was gung ho and ready to tackle whatever was necessary to grow those vegetables. So I planted, and I watered, and I fertilized and I watched those seeds germinate and those plants begin to grow. Every day I'd check their status, and when the weeds started appearing, I'd work to pull them all up.

But there were days I just couldn't get to them. I'd be out of town or really busy with another project. My boys were little so I had lots of responsibility. And what happened over those few days? The weeds began to overtake my garden and quickly became more than I could remove. Then the bugs began to eat my peas and butterbeans even though I sprayed them with insecticide. And I let my squash get too big to eat. I determined that the weeds and bugs had won. My huge garden was a failure. I reaped very little that year.

My second garden was very recent. This time the beds were very small and above ground and, I thought, easy to maintain. I only grew a few plants and determined to take care of them. The weeds were easy to remove. But guess what? I'd let days go by without checking on that garden because I was busy or I'd forget. And I only fertilized it two times, knowing it needed more than that. Again, I reaped very little.

Do you see the similarity in my failure both times? A garden requires DAILY care, whether it's huge or whether it's small. Bugs have to be dealt with quickly. Fertilizer must be applied regularly. Water must be regulated.

It's the very same with our walk with Jesus.

When we don't begin our day as He did, quiet time alone with the Father, we are letting those weeds enter.

When we don't read the Word daily, we are not allowing the water of the Word to enter our hearts; we are not seeking His Face as we must do.

When we don't pray without ceasing, we are letting those pests enter as we listen to voices in our head that are not of Him.

When we don't praise His precious Holy Name daily, we are not fertilizing the love in our hearts that has to be in a constant state of growing.

THIS is how we endure so much and do not faint: we let nothing interfere with our daily quiet time with Him, let nothing interfere with daily reading the Word, let nothing interfere with daily seeking His face, let nothing interfere with praying without ceasing, and let nothing interfere with daily praising His Name.

DAILY we must care for a garden. And DAILY we must seek His Face.

When I get discouraged, I think of Peter. Peter was there when Jesus told His crowd of followers in the synagogue in Capernaum that unless they ate His flesh and drank His blood, they had no life in them (John 6:53–58). If only they had paid close attention to His words prior to that, they could have understood. Because in the verses preceding, He talked about the food that endures to everlasting life, which HE would give them. He told them He was the bread of God who came down from Heaven and would give life to the world. He even told them that all who would come to Him would never hunger or thirst. He said, "I am the bread of life. This is the bread which comes down from Heaven, that one may eat of it and not die. I am the living bread which came down from Heaven. If anyone eats of this bread, he will live forever; and the bread that I shall give is My flesh, which I shall give for the life of the world." He tried to make it clear.

But they all struggled to understand His words and their meaning. And from that day, "many of His disciples went back and walked with Him no more" (verse 66). So Jesus asked his twelve disciples this: "Do you also want to go away?" (verse 67)

And here it is: "But Simon Peter answered Him, 'Lord, to whom shall we go? You have the words of eternal life. Also, we have come to believe and know that You are the Christ, the Son of the living God.'"

Peter had tasted and seen. He had tasted and seen that Jesus was Lord of all. And he had burned every bridge behind him. Just as we must make the choice to do once WE have tasted and seen Him for Who He is.

As Peter said, where would we go?

I have learned that the things of the world brings only temporary happiness, nothing lasting.

I have learned that the lust of the flesh can never be satisfied, but only longs for more.

I have learned that the only real joy and peace to be found is in the arms of my Lord and Savior, Jesus! Even when life is so difficult, it's the only place to find hope. Even when my heart is broken in two, it's the only place to find comfort. Even when nothing seems to be going as planned, it's the only place to find peace. And why would we let go of hope, comfort and peace to embrace only brokenness, heartache and difficulty? Why would we go from life to death?

Do you remember what Jesus said when He looked over Jerusalem right before He went to the Cross? "How often I longed to gather your children together, as a hen gathers her chicks under her wings, but you were not willing." Have you ever seen a mother hen do this? She spreads those wings out as far as necessary to cover and hold those baby chicks close to her body and her heart. To let them know that they are safe in her arms. THAT is the God we serve.

We all get weary. It's a fact. But fainting is not an option. Walking away from the Giver of Life is not an option. He is THE Way, THE Truth, THE Life.

He did what it took to bring us to the Father; He gave His all.

As Paul said in Hebrews 12:3–4, "Consider Him Who endured such opposition from sinners, so that you will not grow weary and lose heart. In your struggle against sin, you have not yet resisted to the point of shedding your blood." He was letting them know that Jesus HAD given His life, but we have not. He told them that hardships and sometimes even admonishments from the Lord would come to us all since we who are saved are His sons and daughters, and those who belong to Him, He must sometimes discipline. But look at verse 11: "No discipline seems pleasant at the time, but painful. Later on, however, it produces a harvest of righteousness and peace for those who have been trained by it." There it is.

Whether we feel beat up by life or by what we perceive as discipline from the Lord, there is a HARVEST to be gleaned in the end.

So let's determine in our hearts to hold fast and do what it takes to reap that harvest. Oh, my friend, how it will be worth it all one day!

20 – HAVE YOU GOT THE JOY?

Nehemiah 8:10—Do not sorrow, for the joy of the Lord is your strength.

What a wonderful verse! I do love it and quote it often, especially when I need joy so desperately but don't have it. Do you know this story in Nehemiah? Nehemiah, a Jew, was the cupbearer for the King of Babylon, and had received word that the city of Jerusalem was in shambles and the wall destroyed. His heart was broken over the news and, when the king saw his despair, he allowed him to take leave and go back to Jerusalem and rebuild the wall. He faced much adversity, but, after twelve years, had accomplished his goal, along with the help of others. On this particular day, they had a celebration for all the people of Jerusalem. They read from the Book of the Law of Moses and, as the people heard the Word, "all the people wept." And Nehemiah's reply? Do not grieve, for this is a day of celebration! And then . . ." Do not sorrow, for the joy of the Lord is your strength." The Jews were so grateful to have their city restored, and so thankful to hear the words of the Lord that they could only weep. But, on that day, He wanted them to have joy. His joy! So beautiful!

Let's start with the basic question: What is *joy*? It's defined as delight or deep satisfaction. The word *joy* is mentioned 165 times in the Bible; the word *rejoice* is mentioned 192 times. That tells us that it is very important to the Father. And what a wonderful thought that He loves us enough that He wants us to walk in joy.

Genesis tells us that God created us in His own image; so, it makes sense, if He told us to rejoice in the Lord always in Philippians 4:4, that HE is joyful.

To fully understand the joy of the Lord, we need to contrast the word *joy* with the word *happy*. The base word of *happy* is "happen," so we know that *happiness* means a good feeling based upon a happening or a situation. But, if our life's outlook is based upon happenings alone, then, when we have a good day, we are happy; when we have a bad day, we are sad. Therefore, happiness is clearly surface and easily affected. But the joy of the Lord, on the other hand, is deep and steadfast. It is based upon our relationship to Him and Him alone. Since He never changes, our joy doesn't have to, either. Since nobody and no earthly thing gave us joy, then nobody and nothing should be able to take it away.

For me, the definition of *the joy of the Lord* is my delight in knowing Him and getting to know Him better each day. It's about being excited about that which makes Him excited. It's about having His heart and His mind about everything. It's all about relationship and walking in obedience. In 3 John 1:4, the Word says, "I have no greater joy than to hear that my children walk in truth." The apostle John was telling us that his joy came from knowing that his brothers and sisters in Christ were loving their Savior and fulfilling their purpose.

So, why do we need the joy of the Lord?

Because walking in His joy makes us strong when we would otherwise be weak. If the joy of the Lord is my strength, then the flip side of that is that the lack of His joy makes me weak. Have you ever noticed that when you are depressed, you are physically weak? That you suffer from a complete lack of energy and feel drained? But energy seems to accompany joy and excitement. That is because walking in joy, His joy, has the power to make us strong mentally, spiritually, and physically.

Because we can abound in the midst of crises if we have it, since the joy of the Lord is greater than sorrow. 2 Corinthians 8:2

says that "in a great trial of affliction, the abundance of their joy . . . abounded." Acts 16 tells the story of the apostle Paul being beaten and imprisoned in chains, knowing he was facing possible death. Instead of despairing, he actually began to sing and praise the Lord! How was he able to have joy in the midst of such a terrible situation? He knew that Jesus was real, He was his Savior, and that no matter what any man did to him, his future was in Heaven. He said, "For me to live is Christ; to die is gain (Philippians 1:21). Paul had the joy of the Lord, and that joy was with him constantly.

Because our joy affects others for good. Philemon 1:20 says, "Yes, brother, let me have joy from you in the Lord; refresh my heart in the Lord." Wow! It doesn't get any plainer than that! Joy and encouragement are contagious. It's hard to be sad around someone who is joyful. That's why it's so important for us to have regular fellowship with other believers, because we tend to become like that to which we are most exposed. When we spend too much time around others who are negative, it can definitely affect us. So, if you are a negative Nancy or a Debbie downer, stop!

Because it was important to Jesus that we walk in joy. John 16:20 says that He will turn our grief to joy. And 1 John 1:4 says, "These things I write to you, that your joy may be full." Fullness of joy. Not full of grief or heartache or worry or negative thinking.

When I was a child and even a young adult, I was only happy when I had something to look forward to in the future. Do you relate to that? After Christmas, I'd look forward to Valentine's Day which was a big deal at school back in the day. Then, I'd look forward to spring holidays. Then, it might be a trip to the drive-in movies to see a Walt Disney movie while eating those delicious hamburgers and popcorn balls my precious Mama made. Then, maybe a visit to or from a relative. Then, summertime and trips to visit grandparents or family out west. And, of course, there were birthdays to look forward to when we would be celebrated.

But, when one event was over, if I didn't have another to look forward to, I was sad.

We used to sing the song, "I've got the joy, joy, joy, joy down in my heart . . . Down in my heart to stay." If you're even close to my age, you know this song. What a great song it is; a fast, happy song. But singing a song about joy had no power to bring me joy and, indeed, never did.

It was only after I came to know Jesus as Savior and walked many years on the road of righteousness that I came to understand joy and how crucial it is in life. Joy is linked to hope for me. And joy can only be achieved when we live in the moment. When we look down the road to the unknowns, to tomorrow and the possibility of what it could bring, we actually miss the joy of today, the joy that is right before us. I missed many days of what should have been joy by worrying about my tomorrows. And, if I let it, that regret brings me to tears.

So, how do we keep the joy of the Lord?

By praising His Holy Name! The Old Testament prophet Isaiah in Isaiah 61 foretold 700 years before Jesus came, "The Spirit of the Lord is upon Me, because the Lord has anointed Me to preach the good tidings to the poor; He has sent Me to heal the broken-hearted, to proclaim liberty to the captives, and the opening of the prison to those who are bound . . . to comfort all who mourn . . . to give them beauty for ashes, the oil of joy for mourning, the garment of praise for the spirit of heaviness, that they may be called trees of righteousness . . . ." I shared in a previous chapter how these verses came alive to me as I walked through my son leaving for the Army. I was an emotional wreck, weak in body, mind, and spirit. And, as I wept before Him, He told me plainly to put on that garment of praise. As I did, He lifted my sorrow and gave me His joy, just as He promised!

By keeping our minds focused on Jesus and never forgetting how the Bible describes Jesus' view of the Cross. Hebrews 12:2 says, "Let us lay aside every weight and the sin which so easily ensnares us, and let us run with endurance the race that is set before us, looking unto Jesus, the author and finisher of our faith, who for **the joy that was set before Him endured the Cross,** despising the shame, and has sat down at the right hand of the throne of God." Jesus was able to look past the horrific suffering and shame of the Cross to the joy that awaited Him thereafter. He knew that His death and resurrection would bring about the salvation of many and was willing to count it all joy to bring us into fellowship with the Father.

Here's what I know: The closer I am to Jesus, the more time I spend in His Presence, the more joy I have! Can you be singing and praising Him as your Savior and not let His joy spill over into your heart? I don't think so.

So, if you don't have the joy today, I pray you will run to the Source of joy, the Creator of joy itself! He is waiting with open arms to bring you His joy! Jesus!

21 – WE ARE THE FRAGRANCE OF CHRIST

2 Corinthians 2:14–18—Now thanks be to God who always leads us in triumph in Christ, and through us diffuses the fragrance of His knowledge in every place. For we are to God the fragrance of Christ among those who are being saved and among those who are perishing. To the one we are the aroma of death leading to death, and to the other the aroma of life leading to life. And who is sufficient for these things? For we are not, as so many, peddling the word of God; but as of sincerity, but as from God, we speak in the sight of God in Christ.

How awesome is it to know that God chose to use us to bring the fragrance of Jesus to this world? When we are saved, when we are covered by His precious blood, the Father looks at us and sees the covering of His Son over us.

I have actually heard preachers say, "God doesn't need you; He can accomplish His purposes any way He wants to." While the last part of that statement is true, the first part is absolutely false and the truth is this: HE NEEDS US, HE WANTS US, HE CHOSE US!

The apostle Paul who wrote Corinthians has told us here that, through Jesus, the Father always does two things: (1) He leads us in victory, and (2) diffuses the fragrance of His knowledge in every place.

So, let's think about this: How does a diffuser work? Oil is poured in a container, then heat or power is applied that causes fragrance to be emitted into the air. This is exactly how Paul said we are to be for our Lord! As we spend time with Him, as we allow His Holy Spirit to fill us to overflowing, that love, that fragrance, is upon us and is emitted and poured out on others.

What goes in is what comes out! We can't expect beautiful things to come out of us if we don't put beautiful things in!

An empty diffuser can be plugged in all day, but no aroma is emitted.

A diffuser full of old oil that has lost its fragrance can be plugged in, but all fragrance is gone.

A diffuser full of stinky, rotten oil can be plugged in, but only unpleasant odors can go forth.

A diffuser full of fresh, fragrant oil can be plugged in and the whole room is filled with fragrance!

This is how we are as well: If we are empty, we have nothing to keep ourselves going, much less to help anyone else. The old oil represents us if we are just going through the motions—if we feel beat up and stale, and so in need of fresh oil! The stinky oil represents us if we are full of anger, resentment, bitterness, wounds, and selfishness, so that only negativity can come out. But, if we are full of the love of Jesus, filled with His Holy Spirit, that fragrance will *naturally* pour out of our hearts for Jesus onto others—others who so desperately need the hope of Christ that we have.

I will be transparent and admit that I have been all of the above. I have been oh so empty, I have gone through the motions when my heart was too broken or overwhelmed to feel, I have been filled with anger and resentment and negativity. But praise be to God, all for His glory, I have also been filled with His Holy

Spirit, and I pray that His fragrance has been poured out to those I meet.

Oswald Chambers said, "We cannot imitate the disposition of Jesus Christ; it is either there or it isn't."

So, in practical, daily ways, what does the "fragrance of Christ" actually look like?

First, I think it looks like **fruit**. Beautiful, fragrant fruit! The fruit of the Spirit that is! What is the fruit of the Spirit? Love, joy, peace, patience, kindness, goodness, faithfulness, gentleness, and self-control (Galatians 5:22). *God has called us to walk in the Spirit, and a natural fruit is produced from within as we daily seek our God.* As we read the Word, we water that seed that produces that fruit; as we pray, we water that seed that produces that fruit; as we praise and worship our King of Kings, we water that seed that produces that fruit; as we keep our eyes on Jesus and focus on Him no matter what is happening in our life and just stand on His Promises, we water that seed that produces fruit; as we choose to lay down our personal goals and our personal wants and dedicate our every breath to the service of the LIVING GOD being obedient to His commands, we water that seed that produces that fruit.

When people are around us, our Lord wants them to see the beautiful fruit that He produces in us, and for them to deeply desire and go after Him! He wants them to see what they can be if they give their lives to Him!

Second, I think it looks like **service**—the service of bearing one another's burdens. Paul said we are to bear one another's burdens and so fulfill the law of Christ (Galatians 6:2). He said we are to weep with those who weep and rejoice with those who rejoice (Romans 12:15). He said when one of our body hurts, we all hurt. We are to come alongside one another, pray for one another, help one another, encourage one another, and comfort one another.

Verse 15 above says that the fragrance of Christ goes out from us to those who are being saved and those who are perishing. "We are the aroma of death leading to death to one, and to the other the aroma of life leading to life." What does this mean?

It's possible that as people observe our lives, as they observe us walking with Jesus and living a life in His service, they come face-to-face with a choice: Am I going to follow that aroma of life I see her living out, or am I going to choose my way—the way of the world (the aroma of death)?

Paul said in verse 17 that we do not, *as so many*, peddle the word of God, but as of sincerity, as from God, we speak in the sight of God in Christ. The word *peddle* means to sell something for personal gain. Sadly, there are some who seem to use the Word and the ministry for personal gain. But Paul is saying that we sincerely, straight from the Father, speak the truth of Jesus, all for HIS glory and not for ourselves.

How important is the fragrance of Christ to our Father God?

A few years ago, the Lord led me to do a study on this very topic. He took me back to the Old Testament, to Exodus, where He gave Moses instructions on the incense that was to burn in the sanctuary and later in the Temple. It had to be a special blend instructed by the Father, to be used nowhere other than on the altar in the sanctuary. Exodus 30:35 calls the incense "pure/holy."

When Moses went to Mt. Sinai to receive the Ten Commandments, God gave Him details of how they were to live their lives and also a command to build a tabernacle/sanctuary where He could come and be with them. We are even told in Hebrews that this sanctuary was a replica of what is in Heaven! (Hebrews 8:5) How awesome is that? God told Moses not to change one detail of His instructions on this sanctuary and told Moses exactly how it was to be set up and where every single item was to be placed. The altar was to be set up in front of the *veil*—the veil that separated the inner court from the Holy of Holies—the place where the Ark of the Covenant was to sit which contained the Ten Commandments. Above the Ark is where the Father would bring His Presence. On this altar, there was to be a "perpetual" burning of this special incense. Every morning and every night, the priest would burn this incense to the Father and, once a year, sacrificial blood would be placed on the horns of the altar.

The veil represented our inability to go to the Father without the sacrifices, the burnings, and the blood of the lamb. Only the High Priest could approach the Holy of Holies and only once a year.

You will remember that the veil that this altar faced is the very veil that was torn from top to bottom when our Lord Jesus on the Cross said, "It is finished." (Matthew 27:51)

So, I pondered why would an incense altar have to sit right in front of the veil? That "pure/holy" fragrance had to represent something or someone very precious to have such a special place in the tabernacle.

I am CONVINCED that, even then, the fragrant incense that was placed on that altar represented the fragrance of Christ! That, even though the blood of Christ had not yet been shed, the Father would not allow the priest to approach Him without the fragrance of Christ going before him! How beautiful is that?

And so, let's ask ourselves: Are we the fragrance of Christ? Since we have come to know Him as our Lord, as our Savior, are we beginning to look like Him, to draw others to Him? Let's pray right now that we are daily growing closer to Him and becoming more and more His aroma leading to life! Oh Lord, let it be so!

22 – THE STILL, SMALL VOICE

> 1 Kings 19:11–12—Then He said, "Go out, and stand on the mountain before the Lord." And behold, the Lord passed by, and a great and strong wind tore into the mountains and broke the rocks in pieces before the Lord, but the Lord was not in the wind; and after the wind an earthquake, but the Lord was not in the earthquake; and after the earthquake a fire, but the Lord was not in the fire; and after the fire, a still small voice.

Since I was a little girl, I've heard this phrase referenced from God's Word pertaining to the voice of God. In this story, Elijah is in hiding after performing great miracles just the day before. God speaks to him in a gentle whisper or a still, small voice.

I have found this to be true in my life. There are times we hear something in our mind for good—a reminder, an admonition, a warning, an instruction. If we belong to Jesus then the Holy Spirit lives in us and we must listen to that voice. The Bible tells us in John 10:27, "My sheep hear My voice, and I know them, and they follow Me." It should not surprise us that the Good Shepherd would lead us through His tender voice in our heart and mind because He alone created us and knows what is for our best.

Sometimes, we are praying and we hear that still, small voice. Sometimes, we are busy at a task and we hear that still, small voice. In this chapter, I will share some of the times He has spoken to me.

I was in the shower getting ready for church one Sunday morning. That next week, I would be finding out the gender of my first grandchild. I heard the still, small voice say this: "Brian will have a son. He will look just like Brian. You will love him like he's yours, but he won't be." Wow! I was so excited, and immediately said, "Lord, was that You?" I knew it was because along with the wonderful news was an admonition. The following week, Brian called me to tell me the ultrasound revealed they were having a son. I remember telling him I already knew because the Lord had told me!

Another time, I had gone to a women's conference with two of my friends to hear a well-known speaker. We were in a huge coliseum with thousands of people. After the worship, the speaker stood up and began preaching, and suddenly stopped and looked down to someone to her left and said, "I don't mean to hurt your feelings, but you need to be quiet; you are distracting me." Silence overtook the building. We could not believe our ears and were shocked that she had chosen to publicly humiliate this person, for whatever reason. I will admit that it was difficult for me to receive her words after that.

On our way to the car after the meeting, we passed a woman standing outside waiting for someone to pick her up. Tears were pouring down her cheeks and my heart broke for her. With my friends, I walked past her and the still, small voice, said, "Go back." I took a few more steps forward and then turned around and went back. I asked her name, told her how much Jesus loved her, prayed with her, and hugged her. She told me she was a pastor. I told her, whatever was wrong, Jesus would heal her heart. She was so grateful and thanked me.

On our way home, I again heard His voice say this, "That was the woman." I was shocked! The Holy Spirit had led me to the woman who this speaker had humiliated. And the story began to unfold in my mind. This woman had gotten a seat at the front because she was a pastor. No doubt, she was excited to be there and must have been saying "amen" and "preach it, sister," being vocal in her praise, when the speaker singled her out and admonished and humiliated her in front of her friends, other pastors, and thousands of people. I could not fathom a sister doing that to another sister. I could only think that Jesus would NEVER have done that to one of His own. How thankful I was that He had chosen me to bring her comfort in His Name!

One morning, I was sitting at my desk working on payroll. My mind was completely focused on the numbers and nothing else. Suddenly, I heard these words in my mind, "I'm coming back soon," and immediately a weight was laid on my heart. And I do mean a physical heaviness. I KNEW it was the Lord's voice wanting me to pray for the lost, and ACT accordingly to witness and tell others. The weight on my heart lasted the entire day and only left that night after much prayer. The Lord has used this physical heaviness on my heart at times to instruct me, to let me know that HE is speaking to me. Each time, the purpose has been to pray or to take action for Him.

I was getting ready one Sunday morning, just brushing my teeth, when I heard the Lord say this: "Bro. Cecil will give a message in tongues today and you will interpret." WHAT? I was terrified! My response was, "But Lord, I've never done that before. And on a Sunday morning?" It was very rare that we had a message in tongues and, when we did, someone else always interpreted. Not me. I began to pray and pray and finally told the Lord that I was His and would do whatever He called me to do. And peace overtook me.

I was playing the keyboard at the time, so I was sitting there when church started and noticed that Bro. Cecil was not there yet. I thought it was strange because he rarely missed. So, worship time began with no Bro. Cecil. I thought that maybe I had just heard wrong and will admit I was hoping so. After the last worship song, we always closed our eyes and spent time wor-shipping in His Presence. As I was praising God with closed eyes, suddenly out of nowhere Bro. Cecil began a message in tongues! I never saw him enter the building and I had full view of the door! I knew then that I had heard clearly and what the Lord wanted me to do. I opened my mouth and began to speak as He led me. And His word came forth. I was overwhelmed!

One morning, I woke up with a phone number splashed across my mind. The number seemed familiar but I couldn't re-call whose it was. I wasn't ready to get up, but I couldn't go back to sleep wondering whose number it could be. So, I went to the computer and looked it up. It was the number of a friend I hadn't seen or talked to in over a year. I knew the Holy Spirit was tell-ing me to call and check on her that day, so I did. We talked for over an hour. I told her how He had awakened me with her phone number in my mind. She loved knowing that she was on HIS mind!

And then there was the night I was having a Women's Ministry meeting in my home and no one showed. One by one, everyone called and couldn't make it for various reasons. Admittedly, I was pretty outdone. I had cleaned my house spotless, had prepared a lesson, and had cooked a spread for our meal. After the last call came in, I shook my head and said out loud, "I'll NEVER do this again." Without hesitation, I heard this: "Oh. So you do it for THEM." Whoa. The Holy Spirit had just called me out. And rightfully so! I hung my head and smiled and said, "No, Lord. I do it for YOU. And I will do it again." Do you see the difference in the outcome of that night if that still, small voice had not spoken? And if I had refused to be corrected?

Many years ago, my husband and I were having some prob-lems and had been arguing for days. I was headed to church and lashed out at him one last time before walking out the door by saying everything was so bad between us that there was nothing left holding us together but a string. And he replied, "I hope the

Lord knocks some sense into you." I was FURIOUS! How dare he act like I was the problem? I had made up my mind that I was not going to put up with the situation much longer and sat down on the church pew feeling very smug and justified in my decision. After the musicians finished leading worship, they sat down and one of the members of the worship team stood to sing a special. As she began to sing a song I knew, I felt my smugness wane and, slowly, the tears began to fall. I was totally broken before the Lord. Here are the lyrics to the chorus:

When you're hanging by a thread, still you can climb life's mountain,
Though the cliffs are rough and jagged, you can cope,
If you should slip and reach rope's end, you'll find the hem of His garment,
So don't let go of that last thread of hope.

Of all the songs she could have sung that morning, why that one? Why the one that unmistakably spoke directly to the words I had spoken earlier? I'll tell you why: because the Lord loves us so, because He had something I needed to hear, and because He knew it would take something specific to reach my hard heart. How He loves us, my friends! Can we even begin to grasp it?

Sometimes, the Lord will speak to us over small things. One night, I was trying to decide which restaurant to go to for supper. I asked my husband and he said it was up to me. So, I was driving and wondering which of two I would choose when I heard, "Go to Creek Bank Restaurant." Well, I thought it was the voice of my Savior, but wondered why it would matter to Him? I decided to do what I had heard and went to that restaurant. Later that evening, I found out that the other restaurant was closed for the weekend because the owners had a wedding. And it was almost 20 miles farther. I just smiled and said, "Thank You, Lord."

Why does He choose to speak in that still, small voice? I am not sure, but as in everything our Savior does, He knows the best way, the perfect way, the way that we will hear, listen, and hopefully act on what He speaks. In the story from 1 Kings that we began with, the Lord first showed Himself STRONG in the wind, in the earthquake, and in the fire. But, when He spoke, it was with quiet gentleness. Like a loving Father. Elijah saw, he heard, and he obeyed!

I praise His Holy Name that He has not left us alone, that He still speaks to us, His children. May we quiet ourselves, listen for Him to speak, and, as Elijah did, heed His voice!

23 – A MEETING WITH THE SAVIOR

Psalm 37:3–7—"Trust in the Lord, and do good; Dwell in the land, and feed on His faithfulness. Delight yourself also in the Lord, And He shall give you the desires of your heart. Commit your way to the Lord, trust in Him, and He shall bring it to pass . . . rest in the Lord, and wait patiently for Him."

Of all the things I will share in this book, this chapter will be the most important. Many times, the Lord has spoken to me, but none more crucial and precious than this one.

The previous year had been very difficult for our family. We had been through a terrific time of heartbreak and attacks. We were still reeling from the aftereffects. There will always be some situations in your life that you cannot share because they are too private. And there will be others that you MUST share. This story is one that must be shared.

My husband and I were about to take a trip to Tennessee, our very favorite vacation spot. We had been often before and were always full of anticipation before going. But, this time, the Holy Spirit had dropped a very specific word in my heart. The word was this: "I am going to meet you there and tell you great and mighty things you do not know."

What? The Lord was going to meet me there? I was so full of joy and hope and awe that He loved me so much He was going to meet me there! How could it be? Nothing like this had ever happened to me before.

So, very early on our first morning there, I set out with a heavy jacket, a blanket (it was COLD), a pen and pad, and two cups of coffee (of course). Still not sure how I carried all that without dropping it! I wasn't sure where I was going, but I had the assurance I would know the meeting place when I saw it. I walked down the sidewalk by the creek that was right beside our hotel. I felt certain it would be beside the water because on previous visits at other hotels I would sit by the creek and pray. But, as I walked, I saw only briers and heavy growth that inhibited my ability to reach the creek. So I became a bit discouraged, but kept walking, even doubting that I had heard my Savior's voice. To my shame.

I finally came to a busy crossing where there was a bridge that restricted me from being able to see to the other side. I waited and finally was able to hurry across. When I reached the other side, I saw the most beautiful park beside the water, and I heard, "This is the place." It looked like the Garden of Eden to me, it was so breathtaking. There was a picnic table right beside the water, so I sat down and pulled out my pen and pad. (It's so important to me that you see what I saw those days, so I have pictures at the end of this chapter.) It is very difficult to convey what was in my heart in that moment, so instead of trying to recreate my feelings, I will share parts of my writing:

> I have walked this morning, Lord, searching for the place of quiet rest, and I have found it! You had nudged my heart saying that You will speak to me when I find that place—a special spot You prepared that was ready for me—to sit at Your feet,

to be still in the warmth of the early morning sunshine. I am listening to the birds sing and watching the sun glistening upon the water—sights and sounds, reflections of Your beauty. I don't want to miss a thing.

"You lead me beside the still waters and quiet my soul." That verse comes to mind and I am here.

I bask, Lord, in Your holy and awesome Presence! Your beauty, Your holiness, is overwhelming.

I look at the waters gently flowing in front of me and You tell me, this is how our lives as your children must be—we must move, we must be busy about Your work as the undercurrent of Your steadfast love pulls us where You want us to go. I savor Your Presence here. It is what I have longed for.

You turn my head and right beside me is a tree that looks unlike anything I have ever seen. There is a terrible, ugly, gaping hole at the base of the tree where great damage has occurred. But, as my eyes follow the tree up, I see it is thriving, which seems impossible looking at the damage. My first thought is that it should not have survived and yet it has. And right beside it, a beautiful, wild, blooming bush is growing. As I look closer, though, I see the damage has only gone partway through. Then, I walk around to the back of the tree and see a picture that can only be described as astounding. It appears in the shape of an arm extending over and around, holding, protecting, covering.

Through this, You say to me that many of Your children have been wounded in a way that could have been a mortal wound. And yet, You came and stopped the bleeding, and stabilized, and gave strength and beauty for ashes. And though the wound is there for others to see, You receive the glory as the life continues to thrive even more than before under the strength of Your mighty Hand.

Then I look to my right and see a mother duck, so beautifully colored, with a dozen or more chicks following closely behind. They follow her every step until she jumps in the water, and then they hesitate. She swims around and then comes back as if to say, "Follow me, it's wonderful," and, eventually, they did.

Again, I see a picture of our loving Father telling us to follow Him ever so closely. Even when it seems He is taking us someplace uncomfortable, He is wooing us to just follow where He leads.

I see a bird land on a topmost limb. It is stripped of all leaves and pointed. I ask the Father why would the bird land in such a desolate spot and He says it's so she can see, can hear clearly, unhindered by all the limbs. And that is where He wants to take us—so high, higher, that we are unhindered by all the busyness. I am here, Lord.

As I look at the flowing water, You tell me that in some places, it is shallow, and in other spots, it is deeper—that there are rough places and that there are smooth places.

This is life, You say. Sometimes the road of righteousness is hard and hurtful; sometimes it is smooth and peaceful. But always, always, Your Presence is with us to carry us along in Your arms.

"The Lord is my Shepherd, I shall not want." Can I truly get this, Lord? That the striving, the burdens that are ever-present with me, don't need to consume me? That You are my Shepherd, that I am Your sheep, and that You will take care of me and lead me where I should go?

Help me, Lord, to lay it all down today, right here, right now, in this place of beauty, this place of rest! I don't want to carry burdens any longer that are not mine and that weigh down my heart and mind.

It is cold and yet I am so overwhelmed by Your Presence that I do not care . . . As I close my eyes, I feel only the warmth of Your love, and You tell me this is how You want me to be—sustained by Your love within, unaffected by what goes on outside. I submit to Your loving arms and love the beauty of Your majesty.

You show me a tree beside me with a branch that is curved and, as I study it, I see that it started out strong. But thick vines that do not belong have come in and are pulling and weighing it down. I see that, eventually, it will break if those vines are not removed. But the branches underneath it are strong and pointed in the right direction.

This is what happens to us when we allow things in our life that don't belong. We get weighted down and lose our way. We start out strong, but then . . . .

And there is the river birch, planted right beside the waters! That verse comes to mind as you compared us to trees of righteousness planted by the waters of Your love, Your Spirit. It is such a beautiful tree—its bark gets stripped bare exposing the layers underneath. But it is a thing of beauty that stands out from the rest, thriving beside the still waters.

And how often we, Your children, feel stripped and bare, exposed to the elements by the blows of life! And yet, because we are planted in You, Lord, and we draw our strength from You, we thrive and are beautiful for others to behold as they see You in us!

I returned to that beautiful meeting place three mornings in a row. Each time, the Lord spoke to my heart, allowing me to listen and rest in His Presence. I was so sad to leave that last morning, telling my Savior that I felt such peace there. Problems faded in His Presence. And this is what He told me: "There are still problems; you just roll them over to Me here. As I want you to do always . . . My child, I am everywhere. Any place you go and seek My Face, I am there. Just as you thrive in My Presence, so I long for you to come to Me so I can speak truth and life to you. You need only come to Me and I am there."

I left Tennessee with a longing in my heart to stay in that secret, quiet place of rest in my heart. I so desired to hold fast to that peace and hope I experienced with my Savior. And He showed me that it is possible if we will just get alone, shut out all the voices and all the noise, and just bask in His beautiful Presence.

Each time we return to Tennessee, I try to drive by that very special place. And, each time, I pray that tree is still standing because of what it means to me. I have observed it each time differently. Once, I saw that the damage was still the same. Another time, I saw that the damage was worse. And the last time, I saw that most of the damage was gone! There was only a "scar" left of what had been.

Only Jesus can heal what is so very broken. Even a tree. Praise His Name!

I don't know where you are in your walk with Him today, but if you are like so many, you are in a place of being overwhelmed. There is nothing simple about life anymore. The bad reports are everywhere, the problems are unending; one is solved and two more arise. There are so many things out of our control that can beat us up and weigh us down.

But, if you receive anything out of this chapter, I pray it is this: THERE IS TOTAL AND COMPLETE PEACE TO BE FOUND IN THE PRESENCE OF JESUS. AND, GETTING IN HIS PRESENCE IS UP TO US. WE CAN STAY BUSY EVERY MOMENT OR WE CAN FIND THAT SECRET, QUIET PLACE TO BE STILL, TO PRAISE HIM, TO LOVE HIM, AND TO LISTEN FOR HIS VOICE. AND THEREBY BE RENEWED, REPLENISHED, AND REVIVED!

I pray you will seek Him and find that place today!

24 – CHURCH FAMILY

Hebrews 10:24–25—"And let us consider one another in order to stir up love and good works, not forsaking the assembling of ourselves together, as is the manner of some, but exhorting one another, and so much the more as you see the Day approaching."

The term *church family* is not a biblical one. And yet, the concept is referred to often in the New Testament.

Jesus and his disciples lived together. They traveled from one city to the next preaching and healing. They were a family for sure. In the Book of Acts, the early church met together daily. They ate together at each other's homes and worshipped together. They met each other's needs and shared all they had with others. They were most definitely a "church family."

The above Scripture is not a suggestion; it's a command. We *are* the "Church," the Bride of Christ, and we are to be together in His Name, in praise and worship of Him, and to "stir up love and good works" in one another, encouraging one another in the faith. It's so vital in the lives of believers to keep one another accountable, but we cannot do that if we don't even meet together regularly. Christians need to be with other Christians on a regular basis. New believers must get into Christian fellowship immediately; it is crucial for their future.

Remember the verse, "I was glad when they said unto me, Let us go into the house of the Lord." (Psalm 122:1) Our hearts should be set on meeting together as often as we can because we need each other.

Some try to say that watching television pastors is good enough; that it's not important to come together. And, if one is homebound due to illness, that's true. But, for everyone else, it is actually a sin, breaking God's commandment. Our dearest and closest friends should be those within the Body, for so many reasons. The Bible says in Ecclesiastes 4:9–11 that "Two are better than one . . . if either of them falls, one can help the other up. But pity one who falls and has no one to help them up." When we are a part of the right church family, they will be there to help us when we fall. They will pray for us when we are sick, bring us meals when we can't cook for ourselves, run errands when we are down, even help us financially when a job is lost or we are in need. When we lose a loved one, they are there to comfort us.

I've heard this saying all my life: "It doesn't matter where you go to church, just go." That couldn't be farther from the truth. Where we assemble with believers is very important. We should pray and ask the Holy Spirit to lead us to the Body where He wants us. We must be sure that we go where we are being taught spiritual truth, where the Bible is being taught correctly. And the Holy Spirit will lead you there as you pray.

We were not created to walk the Christian life alone. We must have others to talk to, to help us bear our burdens, to hear our stories of heartbreak, and to pray for us. And that, of course, works both ways. We must be there for others' needs.

And, when someone confides in us, we must keep that confidence and not break that confidence.

And my next point is very important. I will preface it by saying that if this applies to you, please do not think of it as a personal attack, because I would *never* use a book of encouragement to discourage! I share this to enlighten you. And I will go so far as to confess that I myself have been on both sides of this.

Here's the issue: Please, be very careful about leaving one church body to join another church body. Hear me out. There are those who leave churches as they would leave a club. They go to one church for a while, but only stay until they find a "better" one. They leave and never look back.

And there are those who get angry or hurt as I did as described in a previous chapter. As you recall, I was about to leave in anger before the Holy Spirit stepped in and stopped me. This should not be so. If we allowed the Holy Spirit to lead us to the church where we gather with our brothers and sisters, we should not leave that fellowship until the Holy Spirit leads us somewhere else. If He does, we must go. But, we should always be mindful of the sadness of those we have left.

Here's the reason it hurts so bad: As you meet together year after year, you truly DO feel like family. And, when someone leaves, it really hurts those left behind. Consider this conversation: "I don't want to be a part of our family anymore. I mean, I know you're my blood sister and all, but I've found a family I like better. They have more money and can make my life better, so, as of today, I'm changing my last name. See you around."

Does that sound crazy? Well, that's exactly how it feels when someone leaves your church to go somewhere else for the *wrong reason*. You feel cast away, like there was never a bond between you, like your love for them was a one-way street. You feel like they surely could not have loved you as you loved them. Does this sound selfish? It's really not. Love lost, fellowship lost, hurts. The wounds from a brother or sister are truly those that hurt the most. We should be very careful in hurting anyone, but especially our brothers and sisters in Christ.

I remember one morning feeling very hurt and broken over wounds from my church family. There was a prophetic word that came to my email daily and, on that particular morning, it said this: "Why do you weep and wail over the rejection of others? For I have not rejected you," saith the Lord. WOW! I was blown away that the Lord would send me such perfect comfort in those beautiful words! It was many, many years ago, but I will never forget it.

You see, our brothers and sisters in Christ should be almost as important to us as our blood family. We are to treat them with love and care. We are to weep with those who weep and rejoice with those who rejoice (Romans 12:15). We are to be long-suffering with our brothers and sisters, not easily angered, and forgiving (Ephesians 4:2). We have been commanded to do these things, and it all begins in the Body of Christ, after our own family.

Paul said he wanted to give the church of Corinth solid food of the Word, but because they argued so much with each other, he still had to give them milk of the Word like babies (1 Corinthians 3:2). They were immature believers. I would go so far as to say it is not okay to get angry with a brother or sister and walk away from the Body (like I almost did). There is one Body, the Body of the risen Christ, and He called for us to be unified, of one heart and one mind, and to love one another as He first loved us.

I will reiterate that this is not for admonishment, but for insight. And that I have stood guilty myself of the very things I have just shared.

There are times when it cannot be helped. Sometimes, a new job is involved, a move is involved. Sometimes, Holy Spirit *leads* us elsewhere. But, unless it is the Holy Spirit speaking to your heart to leave your church family, please, don't do it. The next time you are tempted to walk away from the Body you are with, ask yourself a few questions: Am I wanting to leave because I'm angry or have hurt feelings? Am I wanting to leave because the Holy Spirit is leading me to another group of believers? It's so important that we be *Spirit-led* in all we say and do!

As Christians, our job is to encourage the Body, not walk away from it.

We should never be the reason the Body is fractured.

I have grown to love my church family members as I love my own family. I see it like this: I am connected by blood to my own family; I am connected by the blood of Jesus to my church family. Those are some pretty strong ties there!

So, if you are not a part of a church family, pray for the Holy Spirit to lead you to the right one!

And, if you are a member of a church family, make sure you aren't just attending but *serving* as well in whatever capacity you are called. Ask how you can help existing ministries or how you can help in a new one. We are not to be spectators as the saying goes. We are to be active participators!

And the last thing: Don't just attend your church when you don't have anything else to do. Be FAITHFUL!

And, finally, remember our Lord's command: "Love one another as I have loved you" (John 13:34).

25 – BEAR ONE ANOTHER'S BURDENS

Galatians 6:2—Bear one another's burdens, and so fulfill the law of Christ.

C omforting those who are hurting is a mandate from the Father. But, sometimes, it's truly difficult to know how. Have you ever had a friend who suffered a great loss? Or, who was going through one trial after the other? What did you do? Did you avoid them because you just didn't know what to say? The Word tells us in Romans 12:15 to rejoice with those who rejoice and to weep with those who weep. Clearly, we are to "bear one another's burdens" when our brothers and sisters are suffering.

We can learn so much from the Book of Job by studying the good and the bad his friends did to help him in his terrifying time of need. The Book of Job teaches us how TO bear one another's burdens and also how NOT TO. And know that Job was a real man, referred to both in Ezekiel 14:14, 20 and in James 5:11.

Let's start with the good. The three friends heard that Job had lost all his children, all his possessions, and his health so they made a plan to visit him together. The Word says that as they approached him and saw his physical state, they were so crushed that they tore their clothes and wept. Then, they went and sat with him for seven days in total silence. What incredible friends, right? Up to this point, they were.

How many of us would or could even do this? Go to a suffering friend and sit with them for a week because of the depth of their loss and despair? Not many of us, if we are honest. We are all so busy with our own lives that this would be impossible for most. So, we are led to believe that these were Job's closest friends who sat and shared in his suffering. They were "weeping with those who weep."

They started comforting their friend so well! But, then, they went SO wrong.

Sadly, they began to speak and their words were not words of a friend. Each one of them accused Job of being evil and, therefore, suffering all because of his sin. They compelled him to repent of his sins and turn back to God, so that He could bless him and heal him.

You see, they wrongly equated suffering with only one possible reason: He had to be a sinner who was being punished. They didn't have God's Word as we do, which clearly states that the rain falls on the just and the unjust (Matthew 5:45).

God allows suffering for many reasons. He allows it to refine us. He allows it to make us rely on Him. He allows it to test us. He allows it to cause some to turn from sin to righteousness. And, sometimes, He allows it for reasons that we will not know on this earth. At times, there seems to be no possible reason. As in Job's case.

And this is what Job told his friends. He made it clear that he was not a sinner, that he was a righteous man and that God was punishing him for no apparent reason and he would not say otherwise. He even asked God why He was being targeted. He said that it would have been better if he had never been born. Job would NOT lie about his God. One of my very favorite quotes from Job is this: "I know that my Redeemer lives. And in the end, He will stand on the earth." (Job 19:25) God was being silent during this time, but Job affirmed his belief that he served a *living* God Who would one day show Himself strong for him.

And, then, Job told them that instead of bringing comfort to him, they had added to his suffering. Wow. How sad.

Two times in my life, the Lord has laid the burden of someone else on my heart so painfully that all I could do was sob.

The first time, I was talking to a friend at church and, as I looked into his eyes, I saw such a deep brokenness that it was almost unbearable for me. Nothing like that had ever happened to me before. The burden was so heavy that I had to go to bed after I got home. I finally had to ask the Lord that afternoon to please lift the burden because it was just too heavy.

The second time was similar. I was thinking of one I love who was going through the fire when suddenly I felt the full weight of their heartache upon me. I began to sob so hard that I could barely breathe. Again, I asked the Lord to take it from me because it was just too much.

So, why would the Lord do this? Allow the weight of others' pain to be upon us? I believe and I KNOW it is because He wanted me to pray without ceasing for them. Only He knew the depth of their pain and how desperately they needed prayers, how desperately they needed someone else to help "bear their burdens."

Many years ago, I got a phone call from my precious Mama. She was weeping so hard, I could barely understand her. Two people that she cared about had been murdered. By their son. Unbelievable horror. I was devastated for her and for them. The only way I could help was to pray. I prayed for the family, I prayed for my Mama, and I prayed for understanding.

I'll be honest here. Sometimes I ask the Lord to show me things and sometimes He does. But other times, He doesn't. This time, He did.

He gave me a vision of that son hitting his father. And I saw an angel holding the father as he was being beaten. I believe an angel was with his mother as this drug-addicted son took her life, too. I realized that neither of them was alone. Although the Lord did not intervene to stop the actions that took their lives, He sent His angel to hold them and bring them home to them.

I was able to share this with my Mama, and her broken heart was comforted.

So, what should Job's friends have done? They should have listened to him, cared for him, prayed for him, and encouraged him. They should have told him that they didn't understand why he was suffering, but that he was not alone. I can't fathom being in constant, intense physical and emotional pain and being told by my closest friends that it was all because of my sin. Talk about a burden too heavy to bear . . . .

We know how Job's story ends. The Lord did answer Job. In chapter 40, He answered him with questions. "Shall the one who contends with the Almighty correct Him? He who rebukes God, let him answer it . . . Would you indeed annul My judgment? Would you condemn Me that you may be justified?" And, in the end, Job answered all God's questions with this:

"I know that You can do everything, and that no purpose of Yours can be withheld from You. You asked, 'Who is this who hides counsel without knowledge?' Therefore, I have uttered what I did not understand, things too wonderful for me, which I did not know . . . I have heard of You by the hearing of the ear, but now my eye sees You. Therefore, I abhor myself, and repent in dust and ashes." Such perfect, beautiful brokenness before the Father, isn't it? Even though Job questioned God, he did not lie about Him. But Job admitted he had spoken without understanding. And he was forgiven.

Back to Job's friends. God spoke to them, too, and said, "My wrath is aroused against you . . . for you have not spoken of Me what is right . . . Go to my servant Job and offer up for yourselves a burnt offering; and My servant Job shall pray for you. For I will accept him, lest I deal with you according to your folly; because you have not spoken of Me what is right, as My servant Job has." And so they did.

And, then, we know the story. The Lord restored to Job double his previous possessions when he prayed for his friends.

The Lord God made it pretty clear that we must speak TRUTH when we are bearing one another's burdens. It's NOT okay to speak from our opinions.

And THEN . . . I admit I've missed this part until I sit here writing. "ALL (emphasis added) those who had been his acquaintances before came to him and ate food with him in his house; and they consoled him and comforted him for all the adversity that the Lord had brought upon him." All. That has to mean those friends!

How precious to know that, in the end, those very friends came and did what they *should* have done in the beginning: Console Job and comfort Job. They received admonishment from the Lord Himself and learned a very valuable lesson: It is NOT our job to judge or condemn or try to guess the reason for suffering. God alone holds the answers.

We will never know the answers to many things until we get to Heaven. And I've heard some speculate that we won't need to ask any questions then, because it won't matter anymore. You see, He has promised to dry every tear. And, I believe, the joy we will feel in His Presence will overwhelm everything else. Think of it: WE WILL ACTUALLY SEE JESUS! WE WILL SEE THE FATHER! And forever worship them with all those who have gone before!

Thank You, Lord, for showing us in the story of Job how we are to bear one another's burdens in the midst of suffering. May we comfort others in obedience to Your Word, and our actions bring glory to Your most wonderful Name!

26 – HAVE WE GOT THE LOVE RIGHT?

John 15:12—This is my commandment: Love each other in the same way I have loved you.

In January of 2017, my world was shaken.

My husband had been having issues with his throat for a while and was being treated for an infection. After a few months, he began having trouble swallowing. I knew that was serious so I made him an appointment with a specialist in New Orleans. The doctor walked in, put a numbing agent in his throat, put a tube in to take a look, took it out, and said these words: "You have a tumor in your throat, and I am certain it's cancer."

He then began to share what would follow in the upcoming months of treatment. I felt like someone had struck me and wanted to burst into tears. It was all I could do to hold my feelings inside. We both left there in shock of the terrible news.

Following that, we moved to New Orleans and lived in the Hope Lodge, a wonderful gift of the American Cancer Society. We lived there for two months as he walked through the horrific but necessary treatment. My world, as I knew it, stopped.

If I was awake, I was seeing to his needs: making sure he was taking his meds to keep his pain at bay, getting him to every appointment on time, keeping enough Insure on hand, getting weekly hospital receipts, filing insurance to keep money flowing, keeping his clothes washed, keeping his sheets changed, buying new clothes to replace the ones that no longer fit. He would wake me all through the night because he was sick or bleeding from the radiation that had burned his skin so badly. My life changed drastically as I fought with him for his life.

I realized quickly there was only one way to make it through those days. So, I would start my day early with the Lord in a beautiful, screened-in porch there at the lodge with my coffee, my Bible, my phone for praise music, and my pen and pad. I would cry out to Him during those mornings to save my husband's life, to give me strength and peace, and endurance to just make it through the day. And, in His great and mighty love for me, He answered my prayers and supplied those needs.

In the midst of it all, I witnessed human suffering on a constant, daily basis. Every appointment, every day, I saw the terrific suffering of Billy and others. And it changes you. Your perspective changes. What used to bother you before now seems petty. You are no longer battling bad attitudes or minor issues, you are battling life and death.

And, at this point, I'm sure you are wondering what this has to do with getting the love right. I'll explain.

I came to realize during that time that only one thing really mattered at the end of the day, and it was the question this chapter is named: *Have we got the love right?* Love for our Savior, love for others. Because there will come a day for each of us that our answer to that question will mean everything.

Shortly before my precious Daddy passed from earth to Heaven, he said this to me: "God is love. If we don't know God, we can't know love, because He IS love." I had never heard anyone say it like that before. And, as I pondered over his words, I knew he was right. Real love only comes from the Creator of love, the only One Who is able to shed His love abroad in our hearts.

It's actually a sad thing that our English language only has one word for love. We love our family, we love our ice cream, we love our new shoes. And, in my case, I also love my coffee! But, in the

New Testament, in the Greek language, there were four different words for love.

One of those words was *eros,* which is romantic love. Then there was *philia,* which is brotherly love. Love for parents and family was *storge.* And, finally, the most important word for love was *agape.* God alone is the source for this kind of love because it is selfless, sacrificial, unconditional love—the highest type of love. It is the love Jesus has for us that demonstrates through *action.* It is immeasurable, incomparable, and without end.

Wow. Can we even begin to imagine that kind of love? Before He went to the Cross, in the verse referenced above, He commanded His disciples to love one another as He had loved them. With agape love.

We can only have that kind of love, God's love shed abroad in our hearts, if we know Jesus as Savior. When we accept His death on the Cross, when we repent of our sins, when we make that decision, we should change. We should turn from our sins, and begin the process of looking like Jesus daily, by the choices that we make. That's the first step in getting the love right.

So, if we get the love right, what does that look like? And what does it not look like?

If we get the love right, love is going to be what motivates us. Love will be the reason we do what we do. We will seek Jesus first and then we will seek out the hurting just because we know we have what will ease their pain. Small and big acts of kindness in Jesus' Name will make a difference. Sharing the love of Christ that's in our heart, as the Holy Spirit leads, will make a difference. Because of our undying love for the Savior, we will follow His lead and do as He did when He was on this earth. We will go where He says, do what He leads, and then rejoice over having an obedient heart. All because of agape love.

If we don't get the love right, self is going to be what motivates us. Self will be the reason we do what we do. We will seek self first and if there's any time left over, we might think of others.

We will say one thing and we will do another. When someone hurts us, we will repay evil with evil like the world does instead of forgiving. And, sadly, we can NEVER compel anyone else to serve Him because we have failed in our love walk. And it's why Christians are routinely called hypocrites. It should not be so.

When I was in New Orleans during those two months with my husband, at the beginning, I wanted to be alone. I was so sad. I was afraid to leave Billy alone in the room, so, while he slept, I sat on my bed and cried a lot. He actually got so irritated with me that he told me I needed to go home, which, of course, I would not. My sweet Mama asked me when we talked if I had met anyone at the lodge, and I said no, I wasn't really interested. In her great wisdom, she knew that was exactly what I needed. After only a few days and my conversation with her, I knew one of the purposes of my being there was not to withdraw, but to disperse the love and hope of Jesus wherever I, as His daughter was allowed to be, no matter what I was going through. The call on my life had not changed.

So, I began to go downstairs while Billy slept, knowing he could call me if he needed me. I began to go out of my way to speak to new people as they arrived at the lodge, to introduce myself and to share helpful tips. Before I knew it, I had many friends. As situations arose, I was able to ask if I could pray with them, and they always said yes. I spent many hours downstairs as Billy slept upstairs just talking and listening with the hurting.

Some nights, different organizations and churches would come and bring us supper. One night, a group of church ladies came and brought a meal. As I thanked them for their kindness, they asked me the question we always got: "Are you the patient or the caregiver?" We all answered that question quite often. I had had an especially hard day emotionally and, as we talked, they could tell that I was hurting. So, they asked ME if they could pray for ME. And, of course, I said yes.

I realized that night that I was not there just to minister to others, but that I needed to let others minister to me as well.

We had a small chapel on our floor where we could go to sit and be alone with the Savior. It was a beautiful refuge that overlooked the river. One of the men who was there for treatment started a Bible class every Sunday morning. I loved going to hear him sing and share the Word! What a joy that was to feel normal again! His last Sunday before going home, he shared that he would be leaving and that someone else needed to take up the mantle and share after he was gone. I remember thinking, "Don't look at me. My plate is full and I'm not a pastor!" But there were only a handful of us, and he looked straight at me.

The next Sunday was Easter, and I knew in my heart the hurting people there needed fellowship on Easter morning. So, I said, "Ok, Lord, I am Yours. Use me for Your Glory." And on that Easter Sunday morning in the Hope Lodge Chapel in New Orleans, I shared the Easter story and the love of the Savior with those few who came seeking Him. I was so nervous, but I also knew it was His will.

My plan upon arriving at that Hope Lodge was to withdraw.

God's plan was for me to meet with Him each morning during my quiet time, let Him fill me up with what I needed, and then go out and give His love away. And so I did. And that's how I made it through.

So, one more time: Have we got the love right? If not, let's start TODAY! Let's focus on what really matters: loving our Savior and loving others.

When I'm gone, this is all I want others to say of me: "She loved well for the glory of her Savior." That's it!

27 – WISDOM

Proverbs 9:10—"The fear of the Lord is the beginning of wisdom, and the knowledge of the Holy One is understanding."

As the grandmother of eleven precious grandchildren, I am always excited when I get to spend time with them, especially one-on-one, quality time. One recent night, I was blessed to have an incredible conversation with one of my grandchildren on the topic of "wisdom." The amazing thing was that he initiated it, not me.

He shared that he had been unable to sleep one night because of his search and questioning of what wisdom really is. I listened as he spoke of the strong feelings people have on subjects, of how each person is convinced they are right and the other is wrong. In this particular case, he was speaking of a pending election and how very divided our country is. I was so proud of him for seeking truth. And, amazingly, I didn't speak until he finished! At that point, I began to share the story of my search for wisdom and how my concepts and beliefs changed after salvation.

So, what exactly is *wisdom*? Clearly, there is both worldly wisdom and Godly wisdom. *Wisdom* is defined as *"the ability to discern or judge what is true, right, or lasting."* Worldly wisdom will profit only while on this earth; Godly wisdom will carry us here and into eternity with the Savior. So, Godly wisdom is what we must seek!

When I was young and unsaved, my opinions came from my own inward thoughts on various subjects and from my life observations. That being the case, they were always changing just as my experiences changed. As the Bible would say, I was always being tossed to and fro, as the wind. "Then we will no longer be immature like children. We won't be tossed and blown about by every wind of new teaching" (Ephesians 4:14).

But, once I became a believer and started on my journey with the Savior, I came to understand that the Bible is ground zero for wisdom and for truth. As the verse above states, the *fear* (respect, reverence) of the Lord is where wisdom begins. The Word says that the Holy Spirit then leads us into all truth (John 16:13) as we seek Him. And, very simply, if a belief does not line up with God's Word, it is a lie.

If you don't read God's Word, however, you WILL fall for a lie, because you will be unable to perceive or discern truth. Do you know what God hates? Do you know what God loves? As born-again believers, we are to love what He loves and hate what He hates. It's all written in the Book!

Therefore, the way we perceive truth and wisdom is from the lens through which we gaze. Are we looking at the world only through the eyes of flesh or are we looking at the world through God's eyes and God's Word? One will bring us to wisdom and truth. The other will bring us to foolishness and error. Satan has deceived so many as he once deceived me. It is the reason evil seems to be prevailing.

Proverbs 8:17 tells us that those who seek wisdom diligently will find it. So, the key to gaining Godly wisdom is to *diligently* (steadily, painstakingly, continuously) seek! How? Through reading and studying the Word, asking the Holy Spirit to help you block out all distractions; to allow you to focus solely on His voice and His Word. To read and to listen as He speaks to your heart! And He will.

Proverbs 8:11 says that wisdom is better than rubies, and all things one may desire cannot be compared with her. So Godly wisdom is everything! It is better than riches. There is nothing more important in the Christian walk than learning, knowing, and having God's heart on all matters. HIS wisdom.

Proverbs 4:13 tells us to take firm hold of *instruction* (correction), do not let go; keep her, for she is your life. Wow, strong words. So, as we gain Godly wisdom, as we are taught, instructed, corrected by Him, we are to cling tightly to His wisdom and never let it go, because our very life, our future, depends on what we do with the wisdom imparted to us and with the choices we make based on that wisdom.

So, as we seek Godly wisdom, we gain Godly wisdom, and we forever cling tightly to that Godly wisdom!

Godly wisdom was clearly present in the lives of the three Hebrew children in Daniel 3:17–18: "Our God whom we serve is able to deliver us . . . and He will, O King. But if not . . . we will not serve your gods or the golden image." They didn't have a Bible to read from which to glean wisdom as we do. But they KNEW their God in their hearts and their wisdom had come from Him. They had no doubt spent much time in prayer and in worship; they loved Him, they served Him, and they trusted Him, come what may. Their wisdom and love of the Father led them to a choice that forever changed their future and the future of many others who witnessed this incredible miracle! The very Son of God walked with them in that fire! And led them to safety.

So, how does wisdom dictate the choices we make today? And where should God's wisdom lead us? When I am troubled and distressed over the unknown, I have learned to stand on and embrace what I KNOW from His Word. And here is what I KNOW:

I KNOW that the End Times must come just as Jesus told the disciple John in Revelation.

I KNOW that Jesus has gone to prepare a place for those who belong to Him through salvation, and that incredible, unimaginable joy awaits us (John 14:2)!

I KNOW that He has a peace that passes all understanding that we are to walk in as we wait for His Return (Philippians 4:7).

I KNOW that He told us to watch and wait and BE READY for His Return by remaining faithful to Him (Matthew 24:42, 2 Peter 3:14)!

I KNOW that He said the greatest commandment is to love Him with all our heart, soul, mind, and strength (Matthew 22:37).

I KNOW that He said the second greatest commandment is to love our neighbor as ourselves (Matthew 22:39).

I KNOW Jesus commanded us to deny ourselves and take up our cross and fulfill our purpose (Matthew 16:24).

I KNOW that we are to share the Good News with others and, thereby, make disciples of others (Mark 16:15–16).

I KNOW that He said "by their fruits, you shall know them" speaking of who is saved and who is not (Matthew 7:15–20).

I KNOW He commanded us to be joyful always, pray without ceasing, and in all things to give thanks, because He knows that the joy of the Lord is what keeps us strong (1 Thessalonians 5:16–18, Nehemiah 8:10)!

I KNOW He told us 365 times in His Word to fear not, because fear paralyzes us and causes us to stop or, even worse, to retreat.

And each of those I KNOW, I embrace, I believe because I have read the Word and have sat under the teaching of the Word.

So, based on all those things, I am RESOLVED to:

Love and serve my Savior and my fellow man to the end.

Speak the truth in love as led by the Holy Spirit (Ephesians 4:15).

Take every thought captive to the obedience of Christ and not listen for one moment to the lies of the enemy (2 Corinthians 10:3–6).

Praise my Savior on the good days and on the bad days because I KNOW how the story ends!

And then? We do this: Proverbs 3:5–6—Trust in the Lord with all your heart, and lean not on your own understanding. In all your ways, acknowledge Him, and He shall direct your paths.

Now that is wisdom!

28 – GODLY DISCIPLINE

Proverbs 13:24—"He who spares his rod hates his son, but he who loves him disciplines him promptly."

The greatest earthly blessings I have received are my children and grandchildren. I have three wonderful sons and, as of this writing, eleven beautiful grandchildren. I love them all more than I can express and, because of that, I became a mama bear very soon after they were born. I would protect them all with my life without a thought. Because that's what mamas and mama bears do!

The Lord chose me to be the mother of twin boys who were my first babies. And, six years later, He gave us another son. What a joy they were and are! But there's a reason. When that first little rebellion came as a toddler, I knew there must be a response. When they would touch something that could hurt them, and I said no, if they didn't mind, I would pat them on the hand or pop them on the behind. And, throughout their lives when they were disobedient, I responded with discipline. Sometimes that discipline involved a spanking; in their teenage years, it was usually grounding from going out with friends. Proverbs 13:24 makes it clear that loving parents correct their children. But, sadly, not all parents adhere to the biblical principles of discipline.

A few years back, I went to a local department store to make a return. In the line ahead of me were a grandmother, a great-grandmother, and a little girl who appeared to be around four years old. I watched sadly as the child insulted them both, especially the great-grandmother, responding with terrible rudeness each time she spoke. Both grandmothers just smiled as if it was cute. The child's attention turned to me and the woman behind me in the line. She looked back and forth at us, then looked at her grandmother and said, "They're BOTHERING me!" The grandmother looked at me and then back to the child and said, "They're not bothering you," to which she replied, "Yes, they ARE!" I couldn't believe a child was being allowed to insult not only her grandmothers, but perfect strangers. It was clear this child had never been disciplined.

My mind went back to a situation I was in over forty years ago, before I was married. The law firm where I worked was getting new technology and I was being sent to school to train on the equipment. My boss gave me the option of staying in a hotel or with close friends of his, and I chose to stay with his friends. They were a nice couple with a young daughter around the same age of the little girl in the store. At the dinner table, the child reached and got numerous rolls and put on her plate. The dad sweetly told her that she didn't need to get all the rolls. The mom's response to him was something I've never forgotten and it impacted me greatly. She said, "Johnny, LEAVE HER ALONE!" I was mortified that she had insulted her husband in front of me over his attempt to correct the child. After dinner, as we watched TV, the mom kept trying to convince the child that it was bath time. Each time, the child told her "no" and she would wait a few minutes and try again. She finally coerced her with promises of rewards if she would go and take her bath. I was so sad and uncomfortable over the situation and could not wait for my training to be over and return home.

Many years ago, I read a heartbreaking article in *Reader's Digest* of a teenage boy who lived as a male prostitute on the streets of a large city. The writer had interviewed the young man attempting to discern how his life had ended up so broken. Again, I will never forget his response to the reporter. He told him that his mother had never cared what he did. There were never any boundaries as to where he could go or what he could do, and that having no boundaries meant she did not love him. So profoundly he unknowingly shared the biblical truth that BOUNDARIES = LOVE. Children must have boundaries which express love, and when those boundaries are broken, punishment must follow every time and be consistent. It's how they learn obedience. It's how they know that rules are a part of life and are good, and must be followed. Proverbs 23:14 even says punishing with the rod saves a child's soul from hell. Foolishness and rebellion only cease when punishment is swift and decisive.

One last situation comes to mind that I must share. In my party rental business, I had a customer who came in with a young grandson. As we conversed, I watched that child stomp her sandaled feet repeatedly and laugh as he did so. He found joy in hurting his grandmother, and not once did she even tell him to stop. Unbelievable and so very sad for the future of this child.

My boys and I spent many loving hours together as they were growing up. I'd read them books and Bible stories which they loved. We would pray together every night. We went to church every Sunday and Wednesday nights, and they went to church camp in the summer when possible. We spent many an hour outside working on their baseball skills. We went on fun vacations to the beach every summer. They all loved to sit in the kitchen with me, talking as I cooked. They all knew that they could talk to me about anything because they trusted me with their heart. And they knew that they were my heart as well. But they knew, if they disobeyed the rules, they would be disciplined. One of them told me recently that, even though he got his share of paddling growing up, he never once doubted my love. Once again, God's Word confirms this in Proverbs 3: 12, "For whom the Lord loves, He disciplines."

I was most certainly *not* a perfect mother, neither am I a perfect grandmother. The memories of some decisions have caused me much grief and I have had to repent for those decisions. But I raised my children with help from the Word, and Dr. James Dobson, who made discipline very simple and biblical: **You punish a child for willful disobedience. You DO NOT punish a child for being childish (spilling a drink, breaking something).** And you spank a child; you do not beat or abuse a child.

My Daddy disciplined in this way. We four kids knew that he would tell us something only once and that, if we disobeyed, we would be disciplined promptly. He would always hold us after a spanking and tell us how much he loved us, but that obedience was not optional. We never doubted his love, and our home was one of peace.

I pray for all us parents and grandparents today: that we will love our children to pieces, that we will give them lots of hugs and spend quality time with them affirming our love, that we will obey the Word and "teach His words to your children, speaking of them when you sit in your house, when you walk by the way, when you lie down, and when you rise up." (Deuteronomy 11:19) And that we will discipline them according to the Word, knowing that the wisdom of the God who created us is perfect. His ways are always the best ways!

29 – DON'T LET SATAN DISABLE YOU!

Matthew 13:18–22—Listen to what the parable of the sower means: When anyone hears the message about the kingdom and does not understand it, the evil one comes and snatches away what was sown in their heart. This is the seed sown along the path. The seed falling on rocky ground refers to someone who hears the word and at once receives it with joy. But since they have no root, they last only a short time. When trouble or persecution comes because of the word, they quickly fall away. The seed falling among the thorns refers to someone who hears the word, but the worries of this life and the deceitfulness of wealth choke the word, making it unfruitful.

In case you've not lived through this yet, I'd like to teach you about one of Satan's favorite tactics against God's children, the Body of Christ. Our Lord Jesus warned us in the parable of the sower that the cares of the world can choke the Word and we can become unfruitful (and becoming unfruitful implies that we were once fruitful).

If you are saved, absolutely in love with your Savior, walking in the Spirit and obeying His voice, Satan knows that you belong to Jesus. He sees that you are sold out to your Father God, having burned every bridge behind you. You begin and end your day with Him and talk with Him throughout the day, listening for His voice and His Word to speak. He is your forever Beloved! So, how on earth would the devious, wily enemy of your soul attack you?

He determines to disable you. To stop you from being effective. To get you in the pit of despair and heartache and keep you there.

In a previous chapter, I shared about my husband's journey with cancer. When we first met with his chemo oncologist, he explained the effects of chemo and used a word I had heard but did not know the exact meaning. The word was *cumulative*. He told us that the effects of chemo on the body were cumulative. He said that the first few treatments caused almost no issues and you'd think the path was going to be easy. And then he said one day the effects will hit you and it will be harsh. You will begin to suffer and it will not get better until the treatments are over.

That was hard to hear! Definitely not good news. But it turned out to be true. It was exactly as he said. My husband was doing well after the third treatment and then, suddenly, he was unable to eat. His health declined from there until he got to the other side when treatments were finished.

And THIS is exactly how Satan's attacks on us are. He hits us with one problem after the other. We handle each one with prayer and trust and keep on going. Then, one day, we find ourselves overwhelmed with the accumulation of problems and depression sets in. We just want to sleep because, then, we don't have to think about or face the issues. Tada. The enemy has accomplished his goal.

Sadly, I've walked through this very thing. More than once. When I lost my Daddy, I was overwhelmed with heartache. When I lost my Mama, I was again brokenhearted. When our finances were so bad, there seemed no path or rescue, I was overwhelmed with fear. When my Billy was suffering through chemo and radiation, I was overwhelmed with uncertainty. Many times in my sixty-seven years I have felt disabled. And it's a terrible place to be!

So, what do we do? What is the answer when we wake up one morning or sit down one evening and all we can do is cry? Is there an answer? After all, Satan is pretty powerful, right? Can we really fight against him and win?

We most certainly can! And every answer is in God's Word!

Our best example is the apostle Paul. When Jesus first called Paul to be His on the road to Damascus, he told him through Ananias that he would suffer many things for His name. And, he surely did suffer in the years that followed, ending with death as a martyr.

In his letter to the Philippians, in chapter 4, he started by telling his "beloved brethren" to "stand fast in the Lord." Clearly, he knew their lives were hard and knew the enemy wanted them to be shaken by the suffering a life lived for Christ would bring. He then urged them to "be of the same mind" and to help each other. And, then, he said this, "Rejoice in the Lord always. Again I will say, rejoice!"

And THIS is the first step to escaping that pit of despair: PRAISE! When your heart is breaking over life's problems, praise Him, sing to Him, and bless His holy name. That's what I believe the sacrifice of praise must be. Praising Him out of our brokenness, knowing that He alone can lift us up and set our feet on that Rock again.

He also told us in verse 6 to "be anxious for nothing, but in everything by prayer and supplication, with thanksgiving, let your requests be made known to God; and the peace of God which surpasses all understanding, will guard your hearts and minds through Christ Jesus." That is such a powerful verse that it once absolutely changed my life as I came to know that He would guard my broken heart and protect my chaotic mind as I walked through a time of rejection.

Then, in verse 8, he actually told us what we should THINK on! "Whatever things are true, whatever things are noble, whatever things are just, whatever things are pure, whatever things are lovely, whatever things are of good report, if there is any virtue and if there is anything praiseworthy (and there IS ALWAYS A REASON TO PRAISE HIM!), meditate on these things." Wow. We are not to focus on the injustices, the immorality, and the bad reports. We are to focus on good things.

And, then, he told them to "DO THE THINGS THEY LEARNED AND RECEIVED AND HEARD AND SAW IN ME and the God of peace will be with you." Right here, he gave us the key to being at peace, no matter what is going on in our lives. He told them to do as he had done and to follow his example.

My favorite part of chapter 4 follows. He was greatly rejoicing that his friends had aided in his physical needs and thanked them for it. But then he told them this: "I have learned in whatever state I am, to be content. I know how to be abased and how to abound. Everywhere and in all things I have learned both to be full and to be hungry, both to abound and to suffer need." So, we stop here and say how? How had he learned to be content and at peace no matter what he was going through? The next verse answers that question: "I can do all things through Christ Who strengthens me."

Paul's relationship with Jesus was the source of his strength, his contentment, his peace. Jesus was his everything, the reason he lived and breathed. And we know that because his life reflected that! As we read of his comings and goings, his unbelievable sufferings, his writings, we see that he lived out "For me to live is Christ, to die is gain" (Philippians 1:21).

Let's look at a compilation of the things he endured that he spelled out in 2 Corinthians 11:24–27. "From the Jews five times I received forty stripes minus one. Three times I was beaten with rods; once I was stoned; three times I was shipwrecked; a night and a day I have been in the deep; in journeys often, in perils of waters, in perils of robbers, in perils of my own countrymen, in perils of the Gentiles, in perils in the city, in perils in the wilderness, in perils in the sea, in perils among false brethren; in weariness and toil, in sleeplessness often, in hunger and thirst, in fastings often, in cold and nakedness—besides the other things, what comes upon me daily: my deep concern for all the churches." He has told us here of both his extreme physical and emotional suffering, and it is truly severe. He even goes on to tell us "who is weak and I am not weak? Who is made to stumble, and I do not burn with indignation?" Paul was human and he, too, capable, of being overwhelmed.

And yet, he had found the secret was that his life, his breath, his existence, was in loving and serving the God Who had revealed Himself to Him. Paul KNEW that he served a very real, living Jesus, and from the moment he heard His voice, he was never the same again. No matter what he had to endure on the road to Heaven, it would be worth it all to spend eternity with Jesus!

We CAN have that same close relationship with our Savior. We CAN endure all things as we press in to Him. We CAN be victorious over the enemy of our souls who chooses to disable us from being an effective soldier of the Cross. We CAN escape that pit of depression and despair and "run the race with endurance, keeping our eyes on the Prize. As my pastor son, Brian, always says, "It's all about Jesus. From beginning to end, from start to finish, it's all about Jesus." It most surely is.

And so, I thank You, precious Lord, sweet Holy Spirit, for reminding us of this today! I thank You, dear God, for being "the lifter of our head" (Psalm 3:3) when we are low, for telling us in Your Word the beginning and the end of the story, and for creating us a forever home that is so wonderful, it's beyond our comprehension. Until that Day, may we run the race worthy of our calling, looking always unto Jesus!

30 – LET'S GET REAL WITH JESUS

Psalm 139:23—Search me, O God, and know my heart; Try me, and know my anxieties.

There are times in our lives when it seems important to do an assessment of where we are in our journey with Jesus, especially when everything seems to be chaos and confusion.

When we judge ourselves, we are apt to go to one of two extremes: We will either excuse our choices and behaviors and blame others, or we will fall into self-condemnation, neither of which is healthy. We must be honest with ourselves and our Savior in order to profit from this process of knowing where we are and how we are doing on the road of righteousness.

I think the best way to do that is to get alone and pray. Go to your secret, quiet place where no one can enter or interrupt. Then ask the Holy Spirit to quiet your soul, and to speak to your heart. Ask yourself these questions and slowly contemplate each one:

What brings you joy?

What brings you sorrow?

What makes you angry?

What do you look forward to?

What's your favorite time of day?

How often do you sing and praise God with your voice when you're all alone?

Do you spend more time complaining or giving thanks?

Do you spend more time blessing others with your words or tearing them down?

Do you have a good attitude most of the time?

Do you let the cares of the world weigh you down?

Do you feed the desires of your flesh or the desires of your spirit more?

Where does your hope lie? In people? In things? In Jesus?

Could you go one day without social media?

Could you go one day without spending time with Jesus?

Do you set aside a time each day to be with Him?

Which one of these descriptions match your walk with Jesus?

a. Is He an old acquaintance? You used to be close but barely see Him anymore.

b. Is He a casual friend? You get in touch with Him once in a while.

c. Is He a good friend? You care about Him, and see Him fairly often.

d. Is He your best friend? He's your go-to person when you have a problem and you talk frequently.

e. Or, is He the love of your life? Is He your first thought when you awaken? Do you talk with Him all throughout the day, and long for your quiet time alone with Him?

A Place of Quiet Rest is a book written by Nancy Leigh DeMoss about Mary and Martha. If you have not read it, I hope you will. The book is based on the story found in Luke 10:38–42. Jesus was about to have dinner in their home. Martha was busy preparing the meal while Mary was sitting at Jesus' feet listening to Him speak. Martha complained to Jesus that Mary was not helping her. And, we know what Jesus told Martha: that by sitting at His feet, Mary had chosen the best thing.

Martha was more like Peter—impulsive, strong personality, takes charge, while Mary was more like the disciple John—loving and calm, thoughtful. Both men were chosen by the Lord Jesus to be disciples so, clearly, both of their personalities were necessary in the work of the Kingdom.

And, in the case of Mary and Martha, we all know that someone had to do the work. Someone had to clean and cook. So, what Jesus was referring to were priorities, right?

Here's what Jesus was trying to tell Martha: The most important thing is to be with Him—The most important commandment from Jesus' own lips from Luke 27 is to "Love the Lord your God with all your heart, soul, mind, and strength." Because He knows that by spending time with Him FIRST, by seeking first the Kingdom of God, all things we need will be added to us (Matthew 6:33). The more time we spend with Him, the more we will be like Him. Then, we will have His joy, peace, hope, comfort, wisdom, and understanding, all that comes from knowing Him intimately.

When we spend time with Him, and we become more like Him, that projects to other people; they will see His likeness in us. If they are Christians, they can discern our close walk with Him. If they are unbelievers, they can see something different and good in us that they don't understand. And that they hopefully will want. And that you, hopefully, can share with them as the Holy Spirit opens that door. 1 Peter 3:15 says that we are always to be ready to share the reason for the hope that is in us. Revelation 2 is a warning against leaving Him as our first love.

And, then, the second commandment Jesus shared is that we are to love our neighbor as ourselves. We must remember that love is a choice. There are times we must admit to the Savior that some people are hard to love because of their actions against us. But, as I've had to do more than once, I pray that the Lord will give me HIS love for certain others, and that is definitely doable! As we choose to love others with the love the Holy Spirit sheds abroad in our heart, we will want to bless others more than tear them down and help others instead of hinder them.

And so you see, when we CHOOSE to obey those two commandments, the result will be a spillover of His love into all that we are and all that we do. He said in Matthew 22:40 that every single commandment stems from those two! So, if we can obey those two, we can obey them all!

So, now let's honestly assess ourselves. Are we choosing rightly? Are we choosing Him above all else? That's what He's asking us in these questions.

The Lord put a word in my mind as I was doing this study. The word is *nurture.* I just love that word. It brings to mind a mother loving an infant child, holding that child so close. But it also has a spiritual meaning, and it is this:

> To cherish, to further the development of, the process of caring for and encouraging. It's related to the word *nourishment,* that which sustains us.

We MUST nurture our relationship with Jesus. We must cherish, care for, and build our relationship with Jesus. Do you know what the opposite of nurture is? To neglect, to ignore, to deprive. When we don't put our relationship with Jesus first, we are ignoring and neglecting Him, and depriving ourselves of that which fills our every need.

As Christians, we are sustained, we are nurtured through our walk with Jesus (the first commandment), and then we are nurtured by fellowshipping with other believers (the second commandment). We are not to be islands to ourselves; the Word is clear on that.

I kept thinking of this phrase: *nature or nurture.* I don't know what that means to you, but here's my thought. We can let nature take its course, do what comes natural and easy, and just let life be; or, we can choose Jesus and then nurture, cherish, care for, and develop our relationship with Him. It's up to us, right?

And, as His children, we need to understand that this is what He requires of us. Being hot or cold is the only option He has given us. And, our precious Savior woos our hearts to put Him first.

My precious Mama gave me a plaque that has been sitting in my kitchen window for many years. Here's what it says: "Marriage is like a garden. It takes a lot of love and a little work each day." So very true. And so applicable to our relationship with our Savior. Remember, we who are saved are the bride of Christ!

The lyrics to this song are a good way to end.

> In the secret, in the quiet place, In the stillness,
> You are there,
> In the secret, in the quiet hour I wait, Only for
> You,
> Cause I want to know You more.
>
> I want to know You, I want to hear Your voice, I
> want to know You more,
> I want to touch You, I want to see Your face, I
> want to know You more.
>
> I am reaching for the highest goal, That I might
> receive the prize,
> Pressing onward, pushing every hindrance aside,
> Out of my way,
> Cause I want to know You more.

I pray you will find that secret, quiet place today. Jesus is waiting!

31 – ARE YOU READY?

Matthew 25:1–13—Then the Kingdom of Heaven shall be likened to ten virgins who took their lamps and went out to meet the bridegroom. Now five of them were wise, and five were foolish. Those who were foolish took their lamps and took no oil with them, but the wise took oil in their vessels with their lamps. But while the bridegroom was delayed, they all slumbered and slept. And at midnight, a cry was heard: "Behold, the bridegroom is coming; go out to meet him!" Then all those virgins arose and trimmed their lamps. And the foolish said to the wise, "Give us some of your oil, for our lamps are going out." But the wise answered, saying, "No, lest there should not be enough for us and you; but go rather to those who sell, and buy for yourselves." And while they went to buy, the bridegroom came and those were ready went in with him to the wedding; and the door was shut. Afterward the other virgins came also saying, "Lord, Lord, open to us!" But He answered and said, "Assuredly, I say to you, "I do not know you." Watch therefore, for you know neither the day nor the hour in which the Son of Man is coming.

I still remember the day the Lord impressed on my heart to do an upcoming women's ministry on this parable. In my spirit I said, "No, Lord, not the parable of the ten virgins, because I don't understand it." But I knew what the Holy Spirit had spoken. So, I could only pray for understanding.

I went to work that very day and, while there, was taking on-line front desk training at the hotel where I work. They were talking about doing our very best in the workplace and then showed a short video. Here's what it said: "211 degrees is hot water, but 212 degrees produces boiling water. Boiling water produces steam which can power a locomotive. The difference in winning and losing is all in our effort and our choices. The only thing that stands between a person and what they want in life is the will to try it and the faith to believe it possible. Belief fuels enthusiasm and enthusiasm explodes into passion."

There it was: PASSION. The Lord literally said to my heart in front of that computer: "It's all about loving Me with a PASSION."

How is *passion* defined? It's an intense, driving feeling or conviction; an object of love. Jesus MUST BE our passion. He said that the most important commandment of all is that we are to love the Lord our God with all our heart, soul, mind, and strength. That's passionate love. Not lukewarm love.

Because lukewarm love never changed anybody's life.

Jesus said that it's not okay to be lukewarm, it's not okay to be complacent, it's not okay to honor me with your lips, but withhold your heart from me (Matthew 15:8).

And to the church of Laodicea in Revelation 3:15, He said, "I know your works, that you are neither cold nor hot. I could wish you were cold or hot. So then, because you are lukewarm, and neither cold nor hot, I will vomit you out of my mouth." We cannot be lukewarm and acceptable before the Father. Why does He hate it so? Because being lukewarm slaps the Father in the face. It says, "I know You died and gave Your all for me, but I don't appreciate it enough to give my all for You."

If we are lukewarm, the world still has a hold on us. The world is talking and we are still listening.

I read many commentaries on this parable and found they were all over the place, clearly based on preconceived beliefs. So, instead, as I prayed for understanding and for the purpose of this study, I knew I was to lay everything aside but what Jesus actually said.

So, what's the setting for this parable? Jesus was talking to His disciples about the signs of His Second Coming and the end of the world as we know it. It's important to note that there are multiple parables on the same subject, right before and right after this one. The theme of them all is the same: we must be ready!

In the parable of the two servants that precedes the parable of our study, the theme is that while the master delayed his return, the faithful servant was doing the work his master had assigned him. But the evil servant began to beat his fellow servants and eat and drink with the drunkards. Jesus said, when the master of that evil servant returned, he would "cut him in two and appoint him his portion with the hypocrites. There shall be weeping and gnashing of teeth."

In the parable of the talents that immediately follows the parable of our study, the theme is that a man gave his three servants different amounts of money (based on their ability), and went on a journey. The first two worked and invested and produced more money for their master. When he returned, he rewarded the first two because they had worked and used the "talents" he gave them to make more. Here's what he said to them, "Well done, good and faithful servant; you were faithful over a few things, I will make you ruler over many things. Enter into the joy of the Lord." But the third servant hid his money in the ground. His master said this to him, "You wicked and lazy servant, you knew that I reap where I have not sown, and gather where I have not scattered seed. Therefore, you ought to have deposited my money with the bankers, and at my coming I would have received back my own with interest. Therefore, take the talent from him, and give it to him who has ten talents. For to everyone who has, more will be given, and he will have abundance, but from him who does not have, even what he has will be taken away. And cast the unprofitable servant into the outer darkness. There will be weeping and gnashing of teeth."

In the parable of the ten virgins, there are ten virgins or bridesmaids who "went out to meet the bridegroom." Jesus calls five of them wise and five of them foolish. Why? "Those who were foolish took their lamps and took no oil with them, but the wise took oil in their vessels with their lamps." So, the five wise ones had taken a separate vessel filled with extra oil other than the oil in their lamps.

Here's the observation of the parable:

All ten of the virgins were together waiting on the bridegroom.

All ten of the virgins had a lamp.

All ten of the virgins slept while the bridegroom was delayed.

All had oil in their lamps.

When the cry came that the bridegroom was coming, all ten arose and *trimmed* their lamps. What does that mean? It means to remove the charred portion of the wick and add fresh oil. But the five foolish virgins said this to the five wise ones, "Give us some of your oil, for our lamps are going out." So, clearly, they had oil in their lamps or it could not have been "going out," but it had burned out while the bridegroom tarried. So, the wise refused to give oil to the foolish and the foolish went to buy more. But it was too late.

When they returned, the door to the wedding was shut. And, when the foolish virgins returned and asked to enter, the bridegroom said, "Assuredly, I say to you, I do not know you." And then this, "Watch therefore, for you know neither the day nor the hour in which the Son of Man is coming."

I can't imagine anything more terrifying than being left behind when Jesus returns for His Bride, the "Church."

Ephesians 5:25–27 tells us that Jesus "loved the church and gave Himself for it, that He might sanctify and cleanse it with the washing of water by the word, that He might present it to Himself a glorious church, not having spot or wrinkle or any such thing, but that it should be holy and without blemish."

The Book of Ephesians clearly spells out what the life of a believer should look like. Paul talks about who the Ephesian Christians were before Christ and who they should be after Christ. He tells them to put off the old man and his former conduct and to put on the new man, which was created in righteousness and holiness. He tells them not to grieve the Holy Spirit, and not to let anyone deceive them with empty words. He says that "no fornicator, unclean person, nor covetous man, who is an idolater, has any inheritance in the kingdom of Christ and God." He goes on to say that they must walk carefully, not as fools, but as the wise, and to seek and understand and walk in the will of the Lord. He tells them to be filled with the Spirit, to worship and sing and praise the Lord, always giving thanks in the name of Jesus.

Does your life look like that? Are you living your life with Jesus as your first love, with a passionate love for Him that overrides every other love in your life?

He has made it clear THAT is what He requires.

It's not about following rules and regulations and bearing heavy burdens and checking every box.

It's not about walking an aisle and getting baptized and continuing the same life of sin as before.

It's about confessing your sin, accepting Him as Lord and Savior, and giving Him your heart, your soul, your mind, your strength, every part of you. It's about loving and serving and listening and obeying His voice. It's about seeking Him early in prayer and praise and the Word and then going out and doing His will for the day. It's about resting in Him and trusting in Him, going where He says to go and doing what He says to do, no matter what the day brings. It's about looking like JESUS.

And, when we fall down, when we sin, we repent and get up and keep walking on that road of righteousness that we are on with our Savior.

I pray with my whole heart, from the depths of my soul, that you will be READY when Jesus returns. I pray that you will not be the one Jesus called the "evil servant, the wicked and lazy servant, the foolish virgin." Because they all missed Heaven.

I pray that when He comes, He will find you that "good and faithful servant." And that He will gather you in His arms and say, "Enter into the joy of the Lord." And so shall we ever be with Him!

32 – MY DADDY, REV. COYT H. JORDAN, JR.

Ephesians 6:2–3—"Honor your father and mother" which is the first commandment with a promise "so that it may go well with you and that you may enjoy long life on the earth."

I cannot possibly close this devotional book without introducing you to my parents. Although they are both gone, passed from earth to Heaven, their legacy lives on in us, their children, in the grandchildren, and truly in the lives of all who knew them. Because to know them was to love them.

February 12, 2019, at 6:00 a.m., my precious Daddy took his last breath on this earth. The pain of his loss was so deep and overwhelming that I struggled to verbalize my pain. Yet, I knew his was a story that must be shared.

My parents moved to Jackson in 2017 to be near us. My Daddy was a retired Methodist pastor who loved the Lord and loved the Church. He loved giving and told me often to never let the church's Lighthouse account get too low without letting him know; he couldn't bear the thought of kids going hungry.

He also loved a good meal. My Billy found out his favorite foods and often took him a meal of Chinese food or Sonny's Barbeque, along with our three weekly newspapers. Daddy would read them from cover to cover. Billy would sit with him for hours listening to his retelling of childhood stories. We were always amazed at his memory and the minute details he could share; we are convinced he had a photographic memory.

As Daddy grew older and began to encounter medical issues, my Mom lived to take care of him. She laid down any right to herself and spent herself caring for him for many years. "In sickness and in health" meant something to her. They celebrated sixty-six years of marriage in July of 2018.

On February 2, Daddy was so weak, he fell and was too weak to stand. He spent ten days in the hospital but we never dreamed his death was imminent until the last few days before he died. After all, he had just celebrated his ninetieth birthday a few weeks before on what he described as "one of the best days of my life." He said he didn't know so many people loved him. When someone is as special as he was, we wanted him to live to at least a hundred. But, the truth is, even then, we wouldn't have been ready to let him go.

As he began to decline and family members came to visit, I watched him speak both blessings and admonition into the lives of his children, grandchildren and great-grandchildren. His final words meant so much to all of us. I could only think of the biblical fathers who did the same on their death beds. And, one day, he said this to me, "I am ready to go, but if the Lord wants to use me to save one more soul, I will stay." To the very end, he was thinking of others.

We four children took turns staying with Daddy and loved that time with him, until he began to be in terrible pain from kidney failure. We then began to pray for God's mercy to take him to Heaven, that place he had longed to be for so many years.

My Mom had told us she had to be with him when he passed away. So, on that morning at 4:30, the nurses came in and told us his BP was very low and that he would not make it through the day. My sister had the wisdom to call my niece who was with my Mom and tell her she needed to be at the hospital by 6:00. I still marvel at that. The sweet Holy Spirit could only have whispered that to her, because my Mom and niece walked in the door a few minutes before 6:00, walked over to my Daddy's side, touched his head and talked to him, and suddenly his breathing stopped. He lived until he heard my Mom's voice one last time.

The pain of his loss has been brutal. As I cried myself to sleep the first few nights and Billy comforted me, I could only say that I needed to find a word to describe how I felt. It seemed as though no word, no adjective, could adequately describe my grief. I am a "word" person, and found myself desperately needing to be able to convey my brokenness. I will confess that I never found that exact word.

You see, this man, my Daddy, had been a major part of my sixty-four years of life, and the thought of his absence was just too much. He had always been there to comfort, to love, to pray, to understand, to assist, to give, and to admonish when the situation called for that. He loved us all and prayed for us all by name every single day. "Sweet Hour of Prayer" was not just a song to my parents; they lived it.

He always made it clear that the most important thing in life was to live for Jesus, to lay down our life for Him, to love unconditionally, and to forgive every offense. The week before he fell, we had a deep conversation as he sat in his chair, looking me squarely in the eyes, leaning towards me, and telling me almost sternly that family was so important and that we must never allow anything to come between us. He said that if anything ever came between us, that it MUST be worked out. He emphasized the word *must*. I agreed.

His relationship with his Daddy, my Pop, was so close; I would say that I've never known a father and son as close as they were. Daddy wrote in a journal that when he was a child, the two of them loved to go for walks in the woods, admiring God's beautiful creation. One day, he said Pop told him they needed to pray, and they knelt down together. As Pop prayed, Daddy said he felt tears falling down his face but was too young to understand.

When he asked Pop about the tears, Pop lovingly replied that those tears were "the way Jesus let you know we were talking each way, us to Him and He to us."

The morning that Pop died, my Daddy was sick and lying in bed. He suddenly felt the softest kiss on his cheek and opened his eyes. There was no one there. He later realized that it was that exact time that Pop passed from this world to the next. Daddy was so comforted by that kiss (he said the Lord had allowed Pop to tell him goodbye) and the full assurance and confidence that Pop was in Heaven, that he never fell into deep grief over his passing. He said, "Why would I grieve so deeply when I know where he is?"

In the depth of my own grief, the Lord brought that story back to my mind. If my Daddy could be brave and strong and completely comforted by those assurances, then so could I. And, although I never found a word to properly express my grief, I was reminded of the word, the Name, I cling to for HOPE, and that is the Name of Jesus. The Name that causes demons to flee, the Name that conquers all fear, the Name that has power to break chains and strongholds, the Name that causes sorrow to give way to joy, the Name that has endless power, the Name that saved my soul. Just that Name. JESUS. And I have been comforted.

Daddy was a beautiful picture of our Heavenly Father, and we miss him terribly. So, we grieve, but we move on. We weep, but we will fulfill our purpose as ordained by our Father God. We stand on the promise that the joy of the Lord is our strength. We choose joy in the midst of sorrow. And we pray, as Daddy did, that the Lord will use us to save one more soul. One day at a time. Until that glorious day that we meet again.

33 – MY MAMA, MARILYN FRENCH JORDAN

Proverbs 1:8–9—"Listen . . . to your father's instruction and don't reject your mother's teaching, for they will be a garland of grace on your head and a gold chain around your neck."

My Mama passed from this world to the next on May 16, 2020. It still does not seem real. When my Daddy passed on February 12, 2019, I struggled to express the depths of my sorrow. It is the same with Mama. It is my honor to give even a feeble tribute to this most precious of women.

Every memory I have of her is of love. I can never remember a moment, no matter how badly I had failed her, when she reacted with anything but love to me. And, somehow, she always seemed to know exactly when I had failed her, even after my best efforts to hide those failures.

One particular incident stands out in my mind. She had agreed to let me go to a dance/party when I was a teenager, but the warning was that I was not to go outside the venue. I was to stay inside the entire time. Of course, I did not obey and went outside with my friends. After I got home, she began to question me (she always knew just the right questions to corner me) about all that took place at the party. When I was unable to answer even the most basic questions, she looked me in the eyes and told me she knew I had disobeyed her. Instead of fussing at me as I deserved, she expressed only hurt and disappointment. This was my Mama.

I remember her letting me have spend-the-night parties often with lots of my friends. Mine were the best because Mama let us stay up all night, play our music loud, and eat the best treats. On one of those nights, the subject of the "facts of life" came up. One of the girls began to cry because her mom had never discussed these issues with her. Mama called the girl's mother and asked if she could talk to her and the mom's reply was, "Yes, please! I just didn't know how to." And so, my sweet Mama, from God's perfect perspective, in front of all us girls, explained it beautifully. Of course, she did. This was my Mama.

After I graduated high school, I took a day trip to the beach with my friends. This was in 1972, before there was such a thing as sunblock. So, my unwise, fair-skinned self fell asleep on the beach from 1:00–4:00 that afternoon lying on my stomach. By the time we got home, I was in terrible shape, crying in pain. Mama made me lie on a rug while she took washcloths and soaked them in ice water laying them on my back and legs for over an hour, trying to alleviate my pain. Which it did. This was my Mama.

As a teenager, I loved my music and especially loved concerts. After one concert in Montgomery where my favorite group had come (The Grass Roots), we asked Mama if we could please go to the motel where they were staying to try to get their autographs. Most moms would have said no, but not mine. She took us to the motel and told us we had fifteen minutes. We found the group outside their room and got autographs and pictures, and were so excited, we lost track of time. I saw someone walking out of the corner of my eye and it was Mama; she just strolled by without identifying herself, letting us know it was time to go but not wanting to embarrass us in front of our music idols. Yes, that was my Mama.

When my babies were born, she came and stayed with me, loving them and helping me care for them as her own. Her choice of names was "Grandma." So, as they were learning to talk, she attempted to get them to say "Grandma," but it came out "Gunga."

She would repeatedly say, "No, say Grandma." But the response was always "Gunga." And so, she became Gunga, not just to her grandchildren, but to almost everyone. I recall someone hearing her being called Marilyn once and saying, "Who is Marilyn? Oh, you mean Gunga."

Through the years that followed, Mama was always there when I needed her. She sat up with me after surgeries, she took care of the boys often, she encouraged me when I was down, she gave of her time and her resources any time I had a need. My sweet, selfless Mama.

They lived in Monroeville for many years. God blessed them with neighbors who were so wonderful they became their adopted children in their hearts. Whatever need arose, these sweet people took care of them. We never had to worry about them with April and Mike next door.

When I found out that they would be moving to Jackson, I admit with great shame that I was worried. I wondered how I would be able to care for them with a plate that was already full and overflowing. I was alone that day on my way to Mobile, and pondered for a long time how my life would change. When I finally let my thoughts go silent, I heard the precious voice of the Holy Spirit say these words, "You've looked at it through your eyes; now look at it through Mine. You will be able to experience the joy of living out their last days on this earth with them." Wow. And, today, I can say that His Words were so true. Caring for them was never a burden; it was a joy and a privilege.

My Billy stepped up and helped me in every way. He would take Daddy a newspaper regularly and sit and visit and listen to Daddy's stories. He would always joke with them and make them laugh like no one else ever could. He would buy their favorite meals and surprise them with a spread of Chinese food or barbecue from Sonny's. He was the source of much joy for them both.

After Daddy's passing, Mama could have withdrawn, stayed at home, and given up. After all, they were married for sixty-six years and she had spent many years caring for him; he was her world. But, instead, she began attending the Jackson Senior Center (God bless those sweet people), went to church every Sunday and Wednesday night, went to the grocery store for herself, still cooked, and lived alone. I was so proud of her. She used to tell me she cried for Daddy every day while sitting in her chair, missing him so. But then, she said, "I get up and go on." That was my Mama.

And my niece Hannah never missed one single night texting Mama after Daddy died. She so looked forward to hearing from her and I am certain it is one of the reasons she was able to go on as well as she did. Sweet Hannah Marilyn, Mama's namesake.

We made so many wonderful memories during her last year. Billy and I took her to Gatlinburg for her first trip there and she loved it so, we had another planned. The Dixie Stampede was her favorite, and she called it "The Dolly Stompede." We still smile about that. She really got into the participation of that night, cheering and stomping her feet with the crowd. Billy later joked her that he could have had more fun except for the crazy lady yelling in his ear. She would always say, "Oh, Billy, you make me laugh."

We had a fun beach trip, grandbaby visits (which were her favorite of all), visits to Bigbee Coffee, and lots of shopping and doctor trips. So many precious memories for which I am so grateful. Precious memories I would not have had they not moved to Jackson. The Holy Spirit is always right and always knows best. Thank you to my brother and sister for making it happen.

A few weeks before she had the stroke, I noticed she was becoming more emotional than usual. Each time I would go to leave her, she would thank me for what I had done and always end with, "I love you so much," and she would start to cry. It was never enough for her to just say, "I love you"; it always had to be "I love you so much!"

Mama had been diagnosed with a heart condition, so we never ended our day without texting and saying goodnight. I was always afraid something would happen to her and she would be alone. Even though she had a medical alert system, we wanted to be sure. So, every night, our message to each other was the same, "Rest well. Love you so much. See you tomorrow."

After she had the stroke, my siblings and I came together to care for her. My sister stayed six days with her in the hospital, never being able to leave her room. She was so faithful. And our two family nurses cared for her when she came home, along with each of us taking turns staying by her side. My Billy was sitting by her when that precious heart stopped beating.

Mama was eighty-eight and lived a wonderful life. She loved us well and was the best Mama anyone could hope for. She adored her grandchildren and great grandchildren, too, and loved spending time with them. She loved Jesus and had a constant prayer life. When one of us suffered in any way, she would cry with us and pray for us. And the older she got, the greater her zeal to be certain everyone was saved. If she thought you weren't headed to Heaven, she would be the first to talk to you and ask you to please give Jesus your heart. She was truly one of the best.

So, now, precious Mama/Gunga, just know that I will never stop missing you, that there is a huge void in my heart that aches to see you. I will weep for you, but just as you did, I will go on. And I will work to fulfill God's calling on my life as we always talked about. No matter what happens to us, we must fulfill that call. I love you so much, Mama. Rest well. And I'll see you one tomorrow in your new Heavenly home.

EPILOGUE

As you have read the foregoing pages, I hope that my prayers have been answered.

I pray that you have come to know Jesus as Lord, if you did not already.

I pray that you have fallen in love with Him and that He is your first love, seeking Him early and giving Him the firstfruits of your time.

I pray that you will let NOTHING come before your relationship with Him all the days of your life.

I pray that you are or will be a part of a church body or group of believers as He commanded.

I pray that you will keep your eyes focused on HIM and not the storms that life brings.

I pray that you will have a merry heart and that the joy of the Lord will be yours.

I pray that the fruit of the Spirit will be evident in your life for all to see.

I pray that you will listen to the voice of the Holy Spirit and be Spirit-led in all you do.

I pray that you will learn to rest in Him and trust Him.

I pray that you will read the Word and know the Word, so that you can stand on His Promises, come what may.

And, lastly, I pray that you will BE READY when He returns! Oh, the joy that awaits us as we spend eternity in His Presence! He said that our minds cannot conceive what He has prepared for those of us who belong to Him! (1 Corinthians 2:9) How we love our Lord Jesus, and long for THAT DAY when we will actually see Him face to face!!

I have prayed for everyone who will read these words.

If you need to contact me, my email address is trishdukes67@ yahoo.com.

CPSIA information can be obtained
at www.ICGtesting.com
Printed in the USA
LVHW081430031022
729845LV00028B/198